Anthony Malpas was born in Sou is
Father Cornish, so he comes fror lis
father's family left Cornwall for W ly
transferred to the midland city of Birmingham.

At a very early age he found that he could travel out of the body and fly about the night sky, visit people sleeping in their beds then return home in the early hours of the morning, none the worse from his Astral Travelling.

As a teenager he experienced many strange and peculiar events which could not easily be explained. Then, in his early twenties his consciousness started to expand even further after studying palmistry, astrology and the tarot.

He originally trained as a professional photographer and was employed in industry, advertising, public relations, fashion photography, the paparazzi and shot documentary movies.

He has written film scripts for the Rank Organization, articles on photography and astrology for many magazines, and published ten books. Then in the early 1970's he set up an astrological consultancy under the title of Golden Dawn Publishing specializing in business astrology. He has lectured to universities and governing organizations, and covered after-dinner speeches on both photography and astrology.

After retiring from the photography world, he has spent the last few years running teaching courses on professional photography, researching many areas of astrology, and writing this book, which will be the first of four unique publications depicting the paranormal.

The remaining three books will cover: Astrology, in a completely unique and different way to the recognized systems; a book on psychic and physical self-defence, which incorporates the ancient Tibetan system of Tumo, including internal body heat transference, to keep warm in cold conditions and protect yourself against psychic and physical attacks. Finally, another unique book on self realization. This will use the tarot to spearhead personal development.

Apart from the above publications he is also currently working on a musical play and has written both words and music.

Blessed Be.

The Multi Dimensional Universe

- A Journey through the Paranormal –

by

Anthony Malpas

*Book cover by kind permission
of
The Archangel Uriel*

to whom this book is dedicated

© Copyright 2006 Anthony Malpas

All rights reserved. No part of this publication may be reproduced, stored in a retrieval system, or transmitted, in any form or by any means, electronic, mechanical, photocopying, recording, or otherwise, without the written prior permission of the author.

Note for Librarians: A cataloguing record for this book is available from Library and Archives Canada at www.collectionscanada.ca/amicus/index-e.html
ISBN 1-4120-9940-4

Printed in Victoria, BC, Canada. Printed on paper with minimum 30% recycled fibre.
Trafford's print shop runs on "green energy" from solar, wind and other environmentally-friendly power sources.

TRAFFORD PUBLISHING

Offices in Canada, USA, Ireland and UK

Book sales for North America and international:
Trafford Publishing, 6E–2333 Government St.,
Victoria, BC V8T 4P4 CANADA
phone 250 383 6864 (toll-free 1 888 232 4444)
fax 250 383 6804; email to orders@trafford.com

Book sales in Europe:
Trafford Publishing (UK) Limited, 9 Park End Street, 2nd Floor
Oxford, UK OX1 1HH UNITED KINGDOM
phone +44 (0)1865 722 113 (local rate 0845 230 9601)
facsimile +44 (0)1865 722 868; info.uk@trafford.com

Order online at:
trafford.com/06-1697

10 9 8 7 6 5 4 3 2

The Multi Dimensional Universe
by
Anthony Malpas

Foreword

When I was a small child I often looked up at the night sky and observed the stars twinkling above. I believed that we came originally from the stars to inhabit planet Earth. I also believed that there were unseen entities, which people called ghosts, flitting in and out of the physical world. Why I should arrive at such beliefs is strange because at that time, before I was five years of age, I could not read, there was no TV and nothing was ever mentioned about the "Multi Dimensional Universe" on radio. Even though my parents were attached to the local Baptist Chapel, they did not discuss spiritual matters, or teach me anything about the possible existence of another dimension.

Around five years of age I started to have peculiar dreams of leaving my physical body and flying about at night, and then in the morning I would wake up in my own bed none the worse for my activities. Every time I placed my head on the pillow at night, a round spinning gateway opened. I would find myself speeding down a tunnel and shooting out into the night sky. I didn't dare to tell my parents, or any other person, in case they thought I was mad and had me committed to the local mental hospital. Years later, when I started to study and understand the metaphysical world, I was able to leave my physical body at will and observe myself lying in bed down below, before zooming off into the night sky.

On many occasions I have been visited at night, not only by living entities, who transferred their consciousness from one side of the world, appearing in physical form in front of me, but also by people who have passed the barrier, left this plane of existence, then returned to tell me that they were still alive. This book is about my personal awareness and journey through the "Multi Dimensional Universe". It is set in the context of a very ordinary life from boyhood to manhood - the background for adventures in the paranormal, which totally changed my perspective on life.

Contents

1	The Multi Dimensional Universe and the 1244 AD Cathar Prophesy	3
2	My Early Years and my first experience of witnessing death.	15
3	Astral Travel and my out of body experiences.	23
4	The Bombing of Birmingham during the war years.	27
5	Return to Birmingham and my psychic visions.	36
6	Astral Vision.	52
7	Transference of Consciousness.	60
8	Does Prayer work? How does it work?	65
9	My Guardian Angel and the sight of my Spirit Guide.	69
10	My father's return from the dead.	75
11	Details of The Multi Dimensional Universe from police files.	80
12	UFO's. Personal contacts.	84
13	Death of a football team. Psychic experiences on a football pitch.	89
14	The Highgate Vampire. My personal experiences of psychic attacks	94
15	Psychological Analysis using Astrology, Palmistry and the Tarot.	109
16	Eclipse. Astro analysis of the greatest ever race horse.	130
17	Organized Religion. How it controls the population?	134
18	Philosophy of accidents. How the cause and effect law works?	139
19	Strange coincidences.	143
20	Why nations and governments fall?	148
21	Astro analysis of the European Common Market. Will it crash?	170
22	Death of a Princess. Was it an accident?	179
23	The ancient Tibetan system of Tumo.	187
24	A modern day witch-hunt.	193

Chapter One
The Multi Dimension Universe

Jesus is reputed to have said, "In my Father's house there are many mansions." His Father's House could be interpreted today as the universe, and the word 'mansions' may have meant dimensions. Who is to say whether this is right or wrong? From my own experiences and observations of life in this plane of existence, plus the strange and fascinating events that have happened to some of my friends, I wonder why so many people denounce the existence of other dimensions as imagination, hallucination, chemical or electrical interference within the brain. If it is true - as Shakespeare wrote - that "There are more things in heaven and earth Horatio, than are dreamt of in your philosophy" – then how can anyone say that a "Multi Dimensional Universe" does not exist?

Every single person will at sometime in their lives experience contact with another dimension, but fear and prejudice will prevent them from examining the facts in a cold and analytical light, so it is much easier to call this imagination or hallucination rather than accept that they were given a glimpse of another reality.

The World of Illusion
The Master Yogis say: "This is the world of illusion and life has much greater significance than is accepted by western philosophy." The ancients knew far more about the "Multi Dimensional Universe" than is taught in western universities and colleges. We in the west leave out many great areas of learning because of fear and difficulties in coming to terms with the idea that we are "Multi Dimensional."

The Scientific Explanation
Scientists inform us that when a vast explosion occurred in the universe, the Sun and planets were formed out of stardust around five billion years ago. Earth was the third planet from the Sun and harboured the right conditions for the eventual development of life. It was not too far or too near the Sun, which turned hydrogen into helium, lighting and heating the Earth.

Then within the Sun's gravity field the planets were slowly formed and solidified as they circled the great giver and sustainer of life. We are led to believe that life, as we know it, originated in the oceans starting with a single cell which changed size, multiplied and evolved. Then the first land creatures emerged hundreds of millions years ago. This started a chain of development culminating in the vast number of life forms on planet earth that swim, crawl, run and fly. How could one single cell eventually develop into a fifty-ton dinosaur? Not only how, but why did it evolve to such a great size? Darwin sold us the theory of evolution which in fact means that life can develop and change, depending on the environment and its urge to survive. So over millions of years, life changed in the physical world depending on the needs activated within each living entity.

Are There Other Dimensions?

If we have evolved from such humble beginnings, is it possible that we could also have evolved in the metaphysical world at the same time, by creating the "Multi Dimensional Universe" ourselves from the necessity to believe in ever-lasting life? Or could there be worlds within worlds, which may have been created by a super intelligence? And are we part of that experiment? Could there be a group of superior beings competing to see who could design the greatest surviving creature on planet earth? Perhaps they have been playing this game all over the universe since time began. Look how the human mind has developed in the last two thousand years. Who is to say what magic will be conjured up by the human race during the next two thousand years? Study the following sentence and see where you fit in the "Multi Dimensional Universe."

The Law of Karma

"Do what thou wilt shall be the whole of the law." To the unevolved this statement could mean that they have the right to do anything they like, regardless of how damaging it can be for the earth or other people. However, to the spiritually evolved it means just the opposite because those who understand the law of cause and effect, or as it is called, the Law of Karma, know that everything returns whence it came. Every deed has a counter-reaction and every word returns to its source, so that nothing can escape the law of God which is perfect. The problem with human thinking is that we expect an immediate reaction from the intelligent energy force that we call God. Look at the evolvement of the human race on this planet. Our known history goes back only a few thousand years yet who is to say that civilizations did not rise and fall then disappear into oblivion millions of years ago leaving no trace that has been found to date in the twenty-first century? When I was young I read an account of a Second World War plane that was found in a wood only twenty years after it crashed with just the wing-tip visible. In a short space of less than half a century, that plane could have been buried for thousands or even millions of years.

The Dead Sea Scrolls, written over two thousand years ago, were discovered in a mountain cave and could have been left there for another two thousand years before discovery. So how old is our present civilization? Look at all the different countries and nations that rose and fell during the last five thousand years and a pattern starts to emerge. When any group of rulers dominate and oppress the people with laws that protect the ruling elite at the expense of the majority, remove freedom of speech, torture and kill those who oppose them, then the law of cause and effect is set in motion. This eventually leads to the destruction of the country, group or religion, who used their power to dominate and control the minds of the people. What happened to the ancient Egyptians, Greeks, Persians, Romans, and later the Spanish, the French under Napoleon, Germany under Hitler, The British Empire, Russia under Stalin, and also (do not forget) the South American Aztecs and Toltecs? Each and every civilization rose and fell because they misused the power they possessed. They activated the law of cause and effect which is the law of God, and whatever they gave out in words and deeds eventually returned whence it came. When war is glorified, and the population is hypnotized into taking up arms against their fellow men, that country will eventually fall. When any dictator instigates the mass execution of a population because they think differently and ask for freedom, that dictator will eventually fall. Any religion that seeks to control the minds of its members by brainwashing the young into taking up arms against their fellow men will eventually fall. Nothing can stop the law of God from operating! The subjugation and removal of freedom from any section of a community will set the cause and effect law into motion. Any country or religion that does not give women the same rights as men will eventually have to change or fall. Whoever heard of a war started by women?

The Devil
Cunning, egotistical and ruthless men always start wars. When tolerance and love are pushed into the background the so-called Devil resides in the minds of men causing all kinds of destruction, as witnessed during the last five thousand years. And today there has been very little change in this male-dominated world. The greatest problem is that governments ignore, or are not aware of, the cause and effect law. They are also oblivious to time. Watch the violent mind-controllers rise up and oppose at every step the enlightenment that occurs, especially when the young become enlightened and respect the law of God.

Will Education Eventually Promote Freedom?
With the advent of computers and emails, within one hundred years from now, almost every person on this planet will have access to information that was thought impossible during the last century. The children of the future will question everything that is happening on this planet and, through future spiritual education, will not so easily fall into the hands of controlling and violent men. So the human race may eventually start to evolve spiritually. Each and every one of us must be very careful not to allow the brainwashing influence of governments or religions to come between God and ourselves. By all means worship the Creator any way you chose but always question the motives of any organization that imposes a mind control by telling you that their way is the right path, and all the others are wrong.

This is the surest sign that they are wrong, not the others!
Always keep an open mind, observe their behaviour pattern, and then analyse the reasons behind their actions. Look for the words of control that will be delivered to you in many different forms. "Follow our teachings and you can be sure of a warm welcome in heaven." In reality this means that you are being blackmailed, making you a slave to their system until death. All over the world there have been many cults calling themselves religious, then brainwashing their members into killing themselves in the false belief that they will go to an everlasting life in heaven. Why do the perpetrators of these terrible

crimes against God not kill themselves? They always pass the buck on to simple well-meaning souls, saying that if they kill themselves, and the opposition, they will go to paradise. These violent, poor, deluded souls often use children and teenagers to do their bidding.

New Scientific Theories of Life

For the last forty years, scientists have been studying a new mathematical system called the *"String Theory"* which they believe could explain the origin of life throughout the universe. It appears they believe that beneath sub-atomic particles that have been observed, then measured through electron microscopes, there is an even smaller substance called strings. Could these be the building blocks of the universe? Also could they account for the formation of not only our physical universe but also a parallel universe as well?

The M Theory

Scientists also found a mathematical formula which they called Theory M. This claimed that it was possible to prove the existence of eleven different dimensions. Some run parallel and others are interwoven within our own dimension, so that one day it may be possible to transfer matter from one dimension to another. Then we may be capable of travelling through time and space so that distances can be accessed faster than the speed of light. Due to my personal experiences since childhood, I have never doubted the existence of a "Multi Dimensional Universe," though when the facts of time and space first intruded into my physical world I assumed that there was something wrong with me; so I kept this information entirely to myself, not even telling my mother and father. The scientists and mathematicians cannot at present prove the existence of the "Multi Dimensional Universe" through a mathematical formula, but who can say that they will not find the answer in the future? A recent scientific TV programme was dedicated to the possibility of time travel, with the theory that time could be manipulated by virtual reality on a computer. We all know that a software programme can be produced indicating past events, present day affairs, then make a future prediction from the information programmed into its database. This means in theory that time could be compressed into one computer programme. So who is to say whether the events transferred on to a computer will not at some time in the future manifest in real life?

The Multi Dimensional Universe   by   Anthony Malpas   7

Do we live in a world of illusion which we create with our own thoughts through the process of imagination? Could we at some time in the future step right through the physical world into a universe of our own creation? Could we be an experiment created by a superior intelligence from another dimension? Also, have we been observed by these intellectual beings for many millions or even billions of years as we stumble from crisis to crisis in the development of the human-race? There is a considerable difference between a mathematical scientist and a philosopher. The scientist demands proof of any theory, which must be repeatedly measured, over and over again in a laboratory. The philosopher lives in a personal world of imagination, so his theories are based on intuition and flashes of insight, sometimes into more than one dimension. The philosopher does not always need scientific proof to believe in a specific theory. However, it is often difficult for some people to bridge the gap between science and philosophy because every great invention or discovery started with a vision or intuition, which was then developed and presented to humanity by the author. Where did that vision come from in the first place? All through my life from a very early age I have lived this incarnation with one foot in the physical world, and one foot in another dimension. While I can understand that the scientific establishment needs to find a mathematical formula which will prove the validity of other dimensions in time and space, I also appreciate as valid the intuition and vision of the philosopher.

The Neutrino Theory

Another interesting development started in 1956 when two scientists, Ray Davis and John Bachall, claimed that they had discovered a particle of matter called a Neutrino. This was an invisible particle with no mass or electrical charge. After years of experiment, they found that Neutrinos did have mass and that one hundred billion Neutrinos passed through our bodies every day making it the essential building material of the universe. Which theory is correct? The String Theory, the M Theory, or the Neutrino Theory? Or could all three be correct? Will scientists eventually be able to demonstrate to the public a practical application of these theories, proving the validity of the "Multi Dimensional Universe?" Only time will tell.

Time travel

One morning I was deep in thought pondering on a specific dream. On looking out of my bedroom window I carefully followed the branch lines of a tree in the garden. The sky was blue and the building opposite reflected bright winter Sun. As I observed the interwoven branches of the tree, I thought about the size of the universe, and how it related to planet Earth. Then I wondered how the universe was formed, with billions of Galaxies, Suns and Planets, all vibrating in a perpetual dance of life and death. How could we ever travel to the other ends of the universe in physical form, let alone to the far reaches of our own galaxy?

The Speed of Light

According to scientists we are physically governed by the speed of light which is 186,000 miles per second, so it would probably take billions of light years to reach the farthest star in our present physical form. However, as I sat up in bed thinking, a picture flashed into my mind of the bedroom wall covered by a large net, similar to the material attached to football goal posts. As I looked closer, I saw the net moving, as though it was caught up in a summer breeze, then it expanded and moved in many different directions. It curved backwards and forwards, as well as sideways, then curved back over itself, with one corner overlapping the centre. Then it occurred to me: perhaps the universe could be manipulated in a similar way to the movement of the net, so that we may never need to travel at the speed of light at all, in order to reach out into the universe. Perhaps the universe was designed to bend with the solar winds and reach out to us. If so, could we then step off from one world or universe and move into another dimension? Could this bring us to a place outside of linear space and time, possibly called the *astral world*, which we also inhabit in our dreams?

Global Dimming

Will the human race survive the next thousand years? We may not even survive the next hundred years, especially if some great tragedy unfolds, such as pointed out in a TV programme called "Global Dimming". This programme suggested that the continued increase of a combination of global warming and global dimming could eventually be disastrous for the majority of people on planet earth.

Pollution from the Past

When I was a boy living in Birmingham in the area named the "Black Country," so called because of the vast number of factories pumping out smoke and dust particles over an area of approximately fifteen miles square, situated between Birmingham and Wolverhampton, I remember the great thick polluting atmosphere, which occasionally smothered Birmingham, and grounded all traffic, with visibility cut down to a few yards in broad daylight so that you could not see the houses on the other side of the road.

On one occasion when I was about six years of age, I went down to the local newsagent to buy a comic. When I left the shop, I perceived an irate milkman holding up a bottle of milk looking for his horse and cart, which had disappeared into the fog. It was nowhere to be seen. However, in the distance we could hear the clop, clop, clop of horse's hooves. Then milkie also disappeared into the fog as he charged after his horse and float. On another occasion there was a football match on Boxing Day, between Aston Villa and West Bromwich Albion at Villa Park. My father, his brother and I went to the ground even though there was a thick fog. We were late arriving, and the match had kicked off, but we could hear the crowd shouting so we paid for our tickets, entered the ground then found a place on the terrace behind one of the goals. Visibility extended for about fifty yards so that we could only see up to the halfway line. Suddenly ghostly figures appeared through the mist. Then the ball was kicked into the air and disappeared from sight. Defenders, opposing forwards, and spectators stared skywards, attempting to anticipate where it was going to land. Then when the ball was cleared, and the players disappeared into the fog. We heard cheering at the other end of the ground, but could see nothing. At half time the fog thickened so much that we could only see up to the eighteen-yard line, and then the game was abandoned.

Because my aunt had a shop within a stone's throw of Villa Park, we all went back to her house, and later that night, my parents and I attempted to walk to the local bus stop to get home to Sparkbrook, which was less than five miles away. The fog was so thick that my father crouched down near the curb striking matches to light the way, and then he walked straight into a lamppost. We gave up and crawled back to my aunt's place and stayed the night. If the effects of this massive pollution had continued, with millions of coal fires and factories pumping out deadly pollution, we would have been in serious trouble long before the twentieth century ended. However, while we have lowered that particular source of pollution, we have at the same time introduced another factor, which may be much more destructive in the long term. Jet engines pump out pollution on a massive worldwide scale; motor vehicles pollute the atmosphere of every big city, probably causing much more pollution than existed in the early twentieth century.

Global Warming Versus Global Dimming

One of the great problems of Global Warming may result in a ten percent or more drop in direct sunlight reaching the earth, due to clouds of ash, soot and sulphur dioxide turning each droplet of pollution into a giant mirror, reflecting sunlight back into space. This causes what the scientists call global dimming, which they claim has changed the rainfall on planet earth because, in the 1970's and 1980's rain disappeared from many regions of Africa causing great drought and famine.

Pollution from Jet Engines

After September 11th all planes in the USA were grounded for three days. The temperature change was enormous! There was a vast drop in global dimming which means that the fuel particles pumped out from the vapour of jet engines travelling around the earth is contributing to global warming on a colossal scale, which in turn increases global dimming. So we have a considerable problem, as we wrestle with the effects of global warming versus global dimming. If on one hand we completely solve the problem of industrial pollution, we may be causing long term destruction from another source with rising temperatures causing more tropical forest fires, also pumping out a vast amount of carbon dioxide.

Destruction of the Rain Forests

Half the rain forests of the world reside in Brazil, and an area the size of six football pitches are destroyed every minute. De-forestation of the Amazon will eventually contribute to an increase of global warming and higher levels of flooding. If and when the rainforest system collapses, the human race will be in serious trouble, because billions of gallons of water which would have been sucked up by the giant forests will eventually flow into the oceans. Then we only need a few massive volcanoes to blow, which could mean that, in one century from now, earth could be five percent hotter. By that time the ice caps in Greenland would have completely melted throwing ten thousand billion tons of methane into the atmosphere. This would eventually mean a sea level rise of over seven meters, with massive winter flooding, and ferocious dust storms in the summer, making half the world uninhabitable.

I wonder which of these scientific theories will prove correct, because one friend said she was visited in the night by an archangel, who stated that 'earth has only a few, short mega-years left'. We are still pondering over the meaning of that statement. Only time will tell.

Follow the course of this book very carefully, and after reading from cover to cover, try admitting that you have never experienced at least a few of the events that I and my friends have encountered. Do not let fear, prejudice, hatred, or ridicule stop you exploring the possibility that there could be more things in heaven and earth than is taught by the fixed scientific establishment and conventional religions. Be free and think for yourself!

The Cathars

The Cathars, who lived in the South of France in the early thirteenth century, were a spiritually advanced civilization that was considered a threat to conventional religion. So the Pope in Rome sent an army of thirty thousand soldiers, under the command of Simon de Montfort, to seek out and destroy the Cathar community. The resulting war lasted about forty years, until all the Cathars were finally destroyed in one last battle. However, many of their secrets and philosophies, that the Pope feared would conflict with the Roman Catholic Church, were dispatched to many countries around the world, and so the following knowledge was saved for future study. After the last of the Cathars was burnt at the stake by the inquisition of the Roman Catholic Church at Montsegur, Languedoc, France in 1244 A.D. they left a prophecy that "The Church of Love" would eventually be proclaimed with the following fabric.

The Cathar Prophesy of 1244 A.D.

The Church of Love has no fabric, only understanding.

The Church of Love has no membership, save those who know they belong.

The Church of Love has no rivals because it is non-competitive.

The Church of Love has no ambition it seeks only to serve.

The Church of Love has no boundaries, for nationalism is unloving.

The Church of Love is not of itself, because it seeks to enrich all groups and religions.

The Church of Love acknowledges all great teachers, who have shown the truth of love, participate and practice the truth of love in all their being. There is no walk of life or nationality that is a barrier. "Those who are. Know."

The Church of Love seeks not to teach but to be, and by being, enrich.

The Church of Love recognizes that the way we are may be the way of those around us, because we are that way too.

The Church of Love recognizes the whole planet as a living being, of which we are a part.

The Church of Love recognizes that the time has come for the supreme transmutation, the ultimate alchemical act of conscious change of the ego into a voluntary return to the whole.

The Church of Love does not proclaim itself with a loud voice, but only in the subtle realms of loving.

The Church of Love salutes all those in the past who have blazoned the way and the light, but have paid the price.

The Church of Love admits no hierarchy or structure, for no one is greater than another.

The Church of Love says that every member will know each other, by their deeds and by their eyes, and by no other outward sign save the fraternal embrace. Each person will dedicate their life to the silent loving of their neighbour, and the environment of the planet, whilst carrying out their tasks, however exalted or humble.

The Church of Love recognizes the supremacy of the great idea, which may only be accomplished if the human race practices the supremacy of love.

The Church of Love has no reward to offer, either here or in the hearafter, save that of the ineffable joy of being and loving.

The Church of Love shall seek to advance the cause of understanding, doing good by stealth and teaching only by example. They shall heal their neighbour, their community and our planet. They shall know no fear and feel no shame, and their witness shall prevail over all odds.

The Church of Love has no secrets, no Arcanum, no initiation save that of true understanding of the power of love, and if we want it to be so, the world will change, but only if we change ourselves first.
All those who know, belong to the Church of Love.

Think very carefully whether the religion that you follow is vibrating on the same frequency as the above Cathar Prophesy.

If you are a seeker after the truth, you will know whether you are following the correct path. It is never too late to change your mind and follow the Church of Love.

Chapter Two
My Early Years

I was born in Mountain Ash, South Wales, in 1932. My mother was Welsh and my father Cornish, so I came from a Celtic background. My father left school at twelve years of age and started work lathering chins in a barber shop, then became a telegram boy, and when he was sixteen, he was employed as a collier working deep underground in the coal mines. In those days hundreds of thousands of men descended into the bowels of the earth, locked into steel cages, which plummeted down at a furious rate. The first time my father entered the cage, he felt a tingle of apprehension when the great pit wheel started turning and the cage gathered speed. It felt as though his stomach was being forced up into his throat. Eventually the cage slowed up and stopped, allowing the miners to clamber out and proceed to their allotted tasks in the maze of tunnels that were channelled under the valleys and mountains of the Welsh countryside. When a shift ended, the miners were transported to the surface, once again to breathe the fresh mountain air. There were no pit baths in those days, so they were covered with coal dust from head to toe. On staggering to their respective homes, wives and mothers filled tin baths with hot water to wash off the grime, which often became ingrained in their skin, and worst of all many ended up with their lungs coated with coal dust. Occasionally a group of miners, all covered with coal dust, would get on to a local bus after a day's work underground, sit at the back of the bus and start singing. I asked my cousin why, and he replied, "After working all day in terrible conditions underground, they were so happy to be still alive, that was why they were singing." Every day the valley floor in Mountain Ash was a hive of activity, as the miners were lowered up and down the pit shaft. Then, like bunnies in a rabbit warren, they proceeded to walk and finally crawl to the coalface, which could often be many miles underground. Pit ponies were harnessed to pull the underground wagons of coal to the loading point, where the black gold was lifted up to the surface. The coal was loaded on to rail trucks, and then shunted backwards and forwards, before being driven off down the valley. The puffing of the engines belching smoke and the clanging of the trucks echoed across the valley between the mountains on either side.

My Uncle Dai was a small thin man with a bald head and a stiff leg. He found it very difficult whenever he went to the cinema, and had to sit on the end seat because his leg was permanently set in stone. His wife, my Aunty Nanna, was a large heavily built woman with a round face. When they were out walking together they were easily distinguished even from a great distance due to the contrast between the thin limping male figure and the rotund rolling woman. Their house was situated half-way up the mountain, and we had to climb up a massive one in four hill to reach the house from the valley floor. My Uncle Dai had a large organ fitted into his front room, and when the windows were open you could hear the strains of Mozart and Handel echoing across the valley. I wonder whether Dylan Thomas based his character "Organ Morgan," on my Uncle Dai. Over the years there were many accidents, with miners killed or severely injured, including my Uncle Dai who was kicked by a pit pony when working underground, the reason for his stiff leg. Later he was offered a job on the surface attending to the coal trucks as they were shunted into position before being driven away by rail to the consumers.

If ever the term 'slave-labour' was typified, it was in the exploitation of the mining community by the landowners, who became rich off the back of the people living in Wales. Uncle Frank, my father's brother, never worked underground, and was given the job of Banksman, which meant that he was in charge of the great winch that lowered the miners down into their underground tombs. This was a very responsible position, because he controlled the speed of the descent, and the return to the surface.

My Father's Narrow Escape
When my father was working in a small seam with another collier he was asked to crawl back along a tunnel about three feet high and bring back a small axe. After crawling about fifty yards, he heard a great roar like a clap of thunder. The ground shook and a huge cloud of coal dust billowed along the narrow shaft, shutting out the light from his lamp and filling his lungs with coal dust. The roof collapsed on top of his friend, killing him instantly. What was it that sent my father back along the mineshaft at just the right time to avoid being killed? Did the other man have a premonition, and was he prompted from within the "Multi Dimensional Universe," to save my father's

life? Without that distance between my father and the coalface when the roof collapsed I would never have been born.

When my father was seventeen, he started learning the violin, and after working all day down a mineshaft, he spent four hours every night practicing. Three years later he departed from the coalface, started teaching the violin and working as a professional musician in the Castle Cinema, Merthyr Tydfil, South Wales. Before he was twenty-one years of age, he was playing the violin in the Ammonford orchestra, which became a winner in the Welsh Eisteddfod. What an achievement for a self-educated boy who left school at twelve years of age, in those very hard times during and after the First World War.

My Earliest Memories

Some of my earliest memories occurred between the age of two and two-and-a-half. Because we lived half-way up the mountain, our back garden rose up well above the roof of the house. After climbing up the back steps, you could look down on the grey slated roof and a smoking chimney. The front of the house, however, faced directly down into the valley, where I could witness the great pit wheel turning and trains shunting backwards and forwards, with the sound echoing around the mountain tops. There was no electricity in our house, just a gas mantle in the living room and candlelight in the bedrooms. Also there was no bathroom or indoor toilet, no double glazing or central heating, and in most houses the bog was a wooden shed situated fifty yards away at the bottom of the garden. If it was raining or snowing on a cold frosty night, silent figures could be seen stumbling along the garden path in sub-zero conditions to end up crouching on a cold wooden seat, with the wind pounding the structure and whistling between the cracks and gaps underneath the bottom of the door. No wonder people suffered with constipation during the early years of the twentieth century.

We were more fortunate because my Uncle John, who was the spitting image of Richard Burton, owned our house and the property next door. In time we had a conservatory built outside the back door leading to our bog, which was situated almost next to the house, so we did not have to walk too far when the wind and rain swept down the valley in the middle of winter. However, every Welsh household sported a guzunda, which was a round china pot about twelve inches wide. When placed under the bed this came in very handy on a cold winter night. The miners had a concession of free coal, which was delivered by horse and cart. It was dumped outside the front door on the pavement and halfway across the road. Then every member of the family hauled great lumps of coal up the entry, and stored the black gold in a special shed, which was filled to the roof. Without this there would be no heating in the house. We had a long, sloping garden with gooseberry bushes, loads of home-grown vegetables, and a chicken pen at the top of the garden.

When I was around two-and-a-half years of age, I remember my mother pushing me into the chicken pen in order to extract the eggs, which was a great adventure for a small boy. I also remember the huge dining table covered with dozens of chicks that had just hatched, scampering backwards and forwards, and then falling off the table with absolutely no physical damage. When the milk was delivered, the milkman just walked into the house through the living room, leaving the bottles on the kitchen table, because the front door was never locked. Burglars and muggers did not exist in those days, probably because every family was in the same boat and there was very little to steal.

My grandfather owned three dry cleaning shops, which he was eventually forced to close because of the great depression in the 1920's and 1930's. Then my father and every other musician playing in the silent cinemas suddenly found themselves out of work when Al Jolson brought out the first talking picture. There was no social security or dole money in those days, so we lived mainly off produce grown in the garden and my father's allotment, just opposite the house. During the depression, when I was about two-and-a-half years of age, the family emigrated to Birmingham because there was very little work or opportunity in the Welsh valleys. Today, when I am lecturing, I always start off by saying that I was born in South Wales, and due to fact that all the pubs closed on Sundays, I left when I was two-and-a-half years old. I could not stand the Welsh licensing laws any longer! That usually goes down well with the audience.

My First Experience of "The Multi Dimensional Universe"

After we settled in the midlands, my first real experience of the "Multi Dimensional Universe" occurred when I was about five years of age during a visit from my Uncle John, who occasionally arrived from South Wales unexpectedly. When we heard his heavy footsteps pounding along outside our house, my mother would shout, "Norman, Edward John is here." Norman of course was my father. Then we all rushed out to greet Uncle John, who on one occasion brought me a pair of brown boots all the way from South Wales. As soon as I tried them on, I went out walking with my Uncle John along the cobblestones of Anderton Road, Sparkbrook, Birmingham, towards Small Heath railway station.

As we walked up the hill, I saw a man staggering towards us on the other side of the road. From a distance of around thirty yards, I perceived that he appeared to be moving in a very irregular way, staggering from side to side, as though he was drunk, and the energy field around him was hardly visible. Most people seemed to have a glow of energy surrounding themselves, just a few inches from their physical bodies, which I could see physically. As he came closer, I noticed that his eyes were glazed, his cheeks hollow, and the entire colour had left his face which was now a deep shade of grey. Then he staggered once more, and fell to the ground with a bang. I knew he was dead because the energy within and around the body disappeared. It did not bother me one little bit because it seemed quite natural that when a life form had ended it simply departed from the physical body. How at that age did I know that a spirit form inhabited a physical body? This was one of my first glimpses in the "Multi Dimensional World". Meanwhile, I continued to live a very ordinary life.

Our house in Birmingham had a long narrow garden with sunflowers on each side of the pathway towering over my head. When it was raining, I dressed up in Wellington boots and a raincoat, then ran up and down the garden in between the giant sunflowers shouting, "It's raining. It's raining." A few doors away, lived a little girl about my age. She also dressed up in rainwear, and then we sang and danced up and down our respective gardens, long before Gene Kelly sang and danced into moving picture history. When the rains ceased, the sunflowers turned their heads and beamed at me, as the rays of the Sun filtered through the clouds with a golden glow, illuminating the garden once more. I felt such a great affinity with our magical garden and those magnificent sunflowers. At the bottom of the garden was a large shed with my swing in the open doorway. I spent many happy hours here in summer, swinging backwards and forwards, gazing with rapture as the great sunflowers were lit by the golden glow from the Sun itself. When I played with a little girl of my own age, I used to frighten the living daylights out of her by telling her all about the ghosts and spirits that were everywhere around us. I have no idea of how I picked up this patter because my parents did not ever mention such matters, there was no TV in those days, and I could not even read. So where did the idea come from that there was another dimension, with entities slipping in and out of the physical world? It just seemed so natural that there were other forms of life vibrating and pulsating, which – I gradually learned - most people could not see.

Playing Truant

When I started school at the age of five, I remember my mother and cousin Muriel taking me around to the local school which was only about half a mile away, leaving me with a teacher and then collecting me later on in the day. I found the years between five and seven were quite magical because I was able to run to and from school by myself every day. I formed numerous friendships with local boys, and one day we decided to play truant from school and go fishing in the local park lake. We spent a glorious afternoon scooping small fish out of the water with a net and then throwing them back into the lake. We could not take them home because our parents would want to know where they had come from. On one occasion as we were walking back from the park with our fishing nets I saw my mother walking down the road towards us. Without hesitation, I hid my fishing net in a nearby front garden, and collected it later.

My friend and I once found a packet of twenty cigarettes, so we sat down and smoked the lot between us. We had great fun pretending to be grown up, whilst puffing away on our little white burning sticks. On returning home I felt very sick and started shaking and sweating My mother looked closely at me, and decided that I was having a bilious attack, so I was sent off to bed, and I have never smoked since that day.

On another occasion we found a silver shilling on the pavement, equivalent to five pence today. We went into a local shop, and during the next few days we lived like kings because back in the 1930's we could buy forty-eight small bottles of what we called pop for one shilling, or forteight gob stoppers, which were large round sweets - so we had a ball.

Annual Holidays in South Wales

Every holiday we went back to Mountain Ash to stay with Auntie Nanna and Uncle Dai for one week. This was all the holiday that my father was allowed. On leaving our house in Sparkbrook we boarded a local train at Small Heath station then changed to the GWR express at Snow Hill in Central Birmingham. The great locomotives were like huge monsters waiting to devour passengers as they poured into the carriages. Then when the doors were shut, the guard blew his whistle and the train slowly gathered speed with great billowing columns of smoke and steam clouding the platform. The wheels spun underneath the great dinosaur and then within a few minutes it was hurtling along the track towards South Wales. I was always impressed with the giant advertising boards at the side of the track as we left Birmingham - two of which always caught my attention. The Guinness ads, depicting various animals; also a long word on one poster site entitled: "The Theosophical Society." The rhythm of the train clattering over the rails was almost hypnotic, and I always went for a walk along the corridor to look out of the windows as we sped through different villages, towns, and stations at a phenomenal speed, until eventually we pulled up in Pontypool station and changed trains.

The small engine then puffed and clanked its way up the Welsh valleys on a tiny branch line all the way to Mountain Ash. There was always great excitement when we neared Crumlin Bridge because it was the highest viaduct in Britain. The train slowed almost to a standstill as the bridge swayed in the wind under the weight of the train, and then slowly chugged its way across the sky. The village down below looked like a collection of dolls-houses. Then as it touched land again, it set off at a fast canter to our final destination. Once we disembarked from Mountain Ash station, we had quite a journey to our old house, which was half way up the mountain. My parents stopped many times, talking to old friends as we hauled the suitcases up the massive gradient. When we eventually arrived, Aunty Nanna would be waving to us as we staggered the last few paces before being welcomed into the house. Next-door was a family with one daughter called Mary. On arrival she would arrange for us to climb up past Ynysybwl all the way to Llanwonno. It was another world which had not changed much since the days of Napoleon. Occasionally there were sheepdog trials and horse racing on the mountaintop above Ynysybwl. Pronounce that if you can? It was a carnival atmosphere with hundreds of local people in attendance. One day, black clouds descended and a mist formed halfway through the trials, then the heavens opened up and if you have never been caught in a thunderstorm on the Welsh mountains you will have no idea of how much rain falls in a very short period of time. We were soaked to the skin and the trials were abandoned. Years later, when I was about thirteen, I was out walking with my mother when we stopped to chat to a woman tending her front garden. She looked me up and down and said: "You are not as good looking as your father. When he was young he looked like a Greek God." I did not look in a mirror for many months, just in case that woman was right.

We went for day trips to Barry Island, Porthcawl and The Mumbles, three seaside resorts within about twenty-five miles from Mountain Ash. Since none of my family could swim, I was not introduced to deep water for many years to come so we just paddled in the sea instead. The fairgrounds and arcades were also a great attraction for a small boy especially the bumper cars and the big dipper. In between trips to the sea and climbing up the mountain we visited friends in the evenings. The week's visit seemed to go like lightning, and then we were packing up and waving goodbye to Aunty Nanna on our way down the valley to the railway station. On boarding the train we always looked out for Uncle Dai who was working on the coal trucks as they were shunted backwards and forwards, before being driven off down the valley. He would always be on the look-out to give us a wave as the train gathered speed on its way back to Birmingham. We returned to my mother's beloved South Wales only once every year. These earthy roots form one aspect of my universe.

Chapter Three
Astral Travel

Is astral travel fact or fiction? The sceptical claim that it is wishful thinking, illusion or a chemical reaction in the brain - also fear of the unknown - often prevents an impartial analysis. Many stage magicians are seen on TV showing the public how easy it is to create so-called psychic phenomena, such as mind-reading, levitation, moving objects, bending spoons and so on. However, for every trick shown to the public could there be an occasional genuine event that cannot be disputed? For instance, not long after that episode of the man dropping down dead, I started to have nightmares, or so I thought because, when my head touched the pillow and I was drifting off to sleep, the room started to spin like a whirlpool. Then a tunnel would appear, through which I would find myself flying - just like the effects created years later in the TV programme Dr Who. One night, I found myself walking along a road, with crowds of people running towards me. Whether they were after me or just running, I did not stop to find out, so I too started running. Then I stumbled and literally lifted myself off the ground, and by a great effort of concentration flew up into the air and perched on the roof of a nearby house. This enabled me to look down at the crowd of people dashing past. Then I leapt in the air and danced from roof to roof, before flying away into the night sky. I could feel the cold night air and the wind blowing in my face and then the next minute I was waking up in bed with my mother standing over me. "What a strange dream," I thought, as my mother got me ready for school.

For many years, the same event happened over and over again! As soon as my head touched the pillow, and the light was turned off, the room started spinning, a tunnel opened and I flew through and zoomed up into the sky like a bird. I looked down and saw houses below me as I flew across the sky. Often, I found myself miles up in the air looking down on a small town, set between large mountain peaks, with lights twinkling in the dark from street lamps and houses. I could see every detail even though I was flying thousands of feet above the earth's surface. Then I would swoop down to ground level and skim over the roof-tops. Once, I found myself flying alongside an aircraft looking at what I perceived were round portholes, through which I could see the faces of people sitting down talking to each other. The plane was a silver colour with two engines, similar to a Dakota. I then zoomed away and found myself waking up in bed the next morning. I never told my parents what was happening because, between the ages of five to seven and a half years of age, I thought there was something radically wrong with me. I still feared that, if I told my parents they would have me put away in an asylum! So Itold no one. Night after night, I experienced the same phenomena until the war started and then, when the bombing of Birmingham intensified, with death plummeting down every night, my nocturnal activities suddenly stopped.

Another interesting memory was that, around the age of seven, I used to do dozens of card tricks. I also acquired a marked deck of cards, so I nearly always won a card game because I could recognize the abstract symbols on the back of each card, and knew what was on the table. Children often love ordinary magic and have an instinct for it.

Out of Body Experiences

I would not have called my early experiences 'out-of-body'. However, years later, I realised that they were just exactly that. I read with fascination accounts of operations being performed in hospital theatres and, whilst the patient was under anaesthetic, they found themselves out of the physical body, able to witness the operation from a position up near the ceiling, seeing and hearing accurately all the events taking place around their physical form.

I have also read many articles from people claiming what is called a near-death experience. There are reliable accounts that many people involved in serious accidents, for example, found themselves either standing outside of their unconscious physical form, looking down on it, or travelling down a long tunnel towards a white light. They would usually meet a deceased relative or other being, who told them that it was not their time to pass on. After that experience, the person would find themselves moving back down the tunnel and waking up in their physical body. Over the years, thousands of people have written about these types of experiences. Sceptics can easily dismiss them as hallucinations. However, medical research is beginning to suggest otherwise.

At present a group of British doctors are in the process of carrying out a scientific experiment in order to ascertain whether consciousness can be experienced independently of brain function. As part of the trial, the doctors set up various visible markers in and around the hospital and its grounds. The aim is to find out whether the patient, while under anaesthetic, is able to travel out of the body, locate any of the items and pass on the required information when awake. It is reliably reported that one unconscious female patient found herself outside the hospital during her operation, at the level of an upper floor. On waking, she reported seeing an old tennis shoe on a high, inaccessible ledge. What was so interesting was that staff had to go to considerable trouble to find the tennis shoe, which was not visible from the window. They did find it. This area of research could be of great benefit to our understanding of the person – that consciousness may not be dependent solely on brain function. It could also conceivably be useful for solving crimes or collecting information during a war. Indeed, the projection of consciousness in this way is already recognised as 'remote viewing'.

Reported Personal Experiences
A 61-year-old playwright from Reading, England had an out-of-body experience when she collapsed after the sudden death of her mother. She found herself in a place that was very bright, like a beautiful summer's day. She asked whether she could see her mother and was taken into a room with a big screen showing people walking across a bridge, including her mother who was wearing a bright pink chiffon scarf. The mother smiled then disappeared into the crowd. She then met a man in this experience who informed her that she had to go back for her son and husband, and but that her husband would be leaving them shortly. Then she crossed a silver bridge and found herself back in her physical body. She felt well and quite normal, looked across the room and found her mother's handbag, which she had brought back from the hospital. On opening it she found the pink chiffon scarf that she had seen her mother wearing when crossing the bridge during her out-of-body experience. The interesting thing here is that the woman had not seen the scarf before, and had no idea that her mother owned one of that colour. Unfortunately her husband developed lung cancer and died two years later, so the prediction she

received from the other side that he would be leaving them was accurate.

Another amazing out of body experience occurred after an armed robbery at a post office. The robbers sped off in a fast car and were trapped in a traffic jam on a motorway. Two police officers arrived at the scene, approached on foot and wrenched open the front door. Then one of the officers was shot in the head with a sawn-off shotgun. He found himself falling down a long tunnel. At the end was a clear blue sky and a fantastic sandy beach - and there was his mother and father, both of whom had previously died.

His father waved and said. "It's not your time son." Then he felt himself hurtling back down the tunnel, and found himself back in the police car, surrounded by colleagues and the arrested robbers. Fortunately, only one of cartridges in the shotgun fired, so the officer was not seriously injured, although he was eventually invalided out of the force.

Another interesting example relates to a car salesman in Doncaster who was working in his showrooms when a fire broke out. Windows and lights were exploding around him and smoke filled the air making it difficult to breathe. Suddenly he saw a very bright warm light at the end of a tunnel and his grandmother was waiting. She smiled, gave him a hug and shook her head. Then he found himself back in his office with the showroom burning furiously. He opened a door that was usually kept locked and walked outside without any form of injury. The showroom was completely destroyed by the fire, but he was unhurt.

Dr Penny Sartori from The Religious Experience Research Centre, University of Wales, is conducting a survey on out-of-body experiences and would be interested in receiving information from members of the public. I would also be very interested in receiving details of personal experiences in this area.

Another chapter will explore this subject further, covering astral vision, transference of consciousness, and returning from the dead.

Chapter Four
Evacuation and the War Years

When the Second World War started I was seven years old. My astral travelling stopped as suddenly as it started probably because my mother decided to send me back to Wales. This was because the area where we lived in Sparkbrook, Birmingham, happened to be very close to the BSA small arms factory which would undoubtedly become a target for the bombers. Because the house that I lived in during my first two-and-a-half years was occupied by my aunt, it was taken for granted that was where I would be staying. However, she was in hospital having an operation and needed weeks to recuperate, so I was billeted out to another member of the family in Mountain Ash. Their house was situated right down in the valley with towering mountains either side. I was sent to the local school. I found the Welsh children of my age well in advance from an educational point of view and, because I could not understand or keep up with the boys in my class, they down-graded me.

Every day on my way to school I seemed to be involved in a fistfight. The Welsh boys thought that I was a Brummie and did not accept me as one of them. However, for the first time in my life I tasted real freedom. No child ever came to harm in the Valleys, so after school and at weekends we all ran around the coal tips and climbed up and down the mountains which were covered with giant ferns and long grasses. When the local cinema ran a horror film, many of the children sneaked in to watch, and afterwards you could hear the howls echoing around the valley as children ran about imitating the cry of the wolf man.

The local butcher was a large fat red-faced Welshman with a very short neck, so he gave the impression that his head started next to his shoulder blades. We called him "Farty Butcher," and danced outside his shop singing the farty butcher song to the tune of John Brown's Body. It went like this: "Farty Butcher's got a pimple on his bum, Farty Butcher's got a pimple on his bum," and so on, until the enraged butcher dashed out of his shop waving a cleaver in his hand and chased the kids away. We had one very simple boy who stuttered, and when I asked my cousin why, he said that Farty Butcher dashed out and caught him by the throat then hauled him into his shop, threw him on the block and then pretended to swing the cleaver to the left and right of his head. The boy eventually escaped and sprinted out of the shop and I was told that he was never the same again. Fortunately for us kids, Farty Butcher was too fat to run very fast, so we all felt safe as we hurtled up the road with Farty Butcher in hot pursuit. I guess he was a great sport and liked the attention and notoriety we gave him. It was a real public relations stunt because every one in the valley was talking about Farty Butcher.

After only six months in Mountain Ash my mother came to find out how I was getting on. She then informed my aunt that she was taking me back to Birmingham because she thought that I was running wild!

Moving House

Before the start of the air raids in the summer of 1940 we moved house and I lost my beloved garden. When I gazed on my beautiful sunflowers and sat on my garden swing, I cried tears of anguish and frustration, as though part of my soul was about to die. When I walked out of that garden and said goodbye to my beautiful sunflowers for the last time tears flowed down my face and I was never the same again. Perhaps when I pass the barrier of the physical world I may be able to create on the astral plane a garden with sunflowers that rise up and never fade. We also had two cats, which produced five kittens, so we were left with seven moggies. Our neighbours took in four kittens and we took the other two cats and one kitten with us, but they always returned to their own sunflower garden which was only about half a mile away. There they lived out their lives in a world that they knew so well. However, the small black kitten named Dinky stayed with us and grew up in our new house.

The Bombing of Birmingham

When the air raids eventually started with the sirens wailing up and down like a colony of cats on heat, we all ran to the Anderson air-raid shelter, which was made out of corrugated iron with a curved roof. A great hole was dug into our garden about six feet deep. The sides, back, and front of the shelter were slotted into the ground, and then the roof was bolted on and covered with earth. There was a narrow entrance which was blocked with a thick wooden door and sandbags were placed around the gap. We needed a small step ladder to descend into the bowels of the earth. Inside we had a couple of double bunk-beds and a small chair, so that five people could at a pinch cram into the shelter. We prayed that we would not suffer a direct hit, though on many mornings we emerged to find houses and factories were destroyed or on fire.

When the sirens sounded, I always grabbed our cat and carried him down the shelter with me. Every person knew the sound of a heavy German bomber because the engine note rose and fell as the plane droned across the sky. Then in the distance we would hear the anti-aircraft guns opening fire, followed by sticks of bombs whistling and screaming as they rained down on us. We could hear the crunch, crunch, crunch of bombs exploding with an ever-increasing noise as they came closer and closer, until the ground shook at every explosion. Great jagged pieces of shrapnel would whistle and thud on and around the shelter. Then, as the bombers passed over, the sound of explosions became less audible as they disappeared into the distance - so we knew that they had missed us on that occasion. Then we waited with bated breath for the next wave to occur. This anticipation of whether we would live or die happened many times every night when the bombers attempted to target the BSA small arms factory.

On one very severe raid, we heard a massive thud and the ground violently shook like a miniature earthquake, as a large bomb dropped nearby. A woman living about six houses away who had run into our shelter for cover, suddenly realized that she had left her ration book in the house as the bombs were raining down. She was most apprehensive regarding the safety of the said document. Our tenant, who was also in the shelter, volunteered to run along the avenue and retrieve the ration book, which was situated in a pantry under the stairs. On his return he was white and shaking. "I went into the pantry and fell over what I thought was a roll of lino. As I was lying by its side it felt cold; then I heard it ticking. When I found my torch and switched it on, I realized it was a time-bomb." The bomb had plummeted through the roof of the house, crashed down under the floorboards, and eventually surfaced in the pantry under the stairs.

The next morning we were all evacuated while the bomb squad defused the brute and took it away. What trick of fate prevented that large bomb from exploding? It would probably have killed everyone in the avenue. During another raid thousands of incendiary bombs were dropped and our house received a direct hit. Because we were living in a terraced house in a small avenue the fire could have destroyed all the other houses. So in the middle of the raid, with bombs raining down, every person in the avenue crawled out of their shelters, and set about dousing the fires in our house. There were incendiaries all over the place, in our front and back garden, and the stairs were on fire. Our main couch was ablaze and an easy-chair was in flames. The only thing we could do was to haul the blazing furniture out of the house into the back garden, and then dozens of men with shovels dug up huge mounds of earth and doused the fires.

There was no water available because the bombing had destroyed all the water mains. The children also participated by digging up earth and smothering the burning incendiaries. To an eight-year-old it was a great adventure. When the all-clear sounded, all the children charged around looking for shrapnel and burnt-out incendiary bombs. The next night there was no air-raid on Birmingham. We came out of our shelters that night, hearing great devastation in the distance. The sky was blood red as exploding bombs and anti-aircraft guns thundered non-stop for hours. Coventry, only eighteen miles away, was that night almost totally destroyed. What trick of fate changed the direction of the German bombers from attacking the area around the Birmingham BSA small arms factory to such a devastating raid on Coventry?

A concentrated raid on the BSA factory would probably have obliterated all of us in the area because the factory was less than half-a-mile away. However, within a few days the devastation returned. All the schools were closed because there was no water, electricity or gas. This meant that all the children in Sparkbrook, Birmingham, were evacuated to different parts of the country.

I was fortunate to be sent to a place called Pinvin near Pershore which was twenty-six miles from Birmingham, and situated in the Vale of Eversham, between the Malvern Hills and Breedon Hill.

When all the children were standing on the railway platform in Snow Hill station, waiting to board the train, I remember my mother asking a teacher where they were taking us and she replied: "This batch is going to Pershore." "Oh my God," my mother replied. "That is in India." "No," the teacher said, "It is in Worcestershire." We were all holding on to our suitcases and our names were written on cards, pinned to our coats. We boarded the train which for all we knew would take us to another world. Eventually we arrived at Pershore station and we were ushered on to the road outside. Then a group of people came up and started to take the boys and girls away to their individual homes. Finally, a very tall, slim and dark-haired woman with a hooked nose arrived, looked down at me and said in a broad country accent, "Be this my evacuee." She grabbed hold and marched me off to her home just up the road at 13 Abbey View, Pinvin, near Pershore. I was introduced to her husband and their son Peter, who was about three years older than me. "This be our evacuee," she said. "We are the Reid family and you will be living with us from now on." I must say that they treated me with great love and respect, though there was absolute discipline in that house.

They were a farming family, and had a massive long garden with apple, pear, plum trees and gooseberry bushes. They grew all their own vegetables and had a vast number of chickens at the bottom of the garden, so there was no shortage of eggs for breakfast, just like it was in Wales. Also we lived next door to the local butcher, which meant that we were supplied with more than our rations of pork and lamb. From there the war ceased to exist, and I spent two-and-a-half years in this rural country setting. There were miles and miles of apple orchards which the German bombers never destroyed. The destruction occurred later when the EEC Bureaucrats brought in their rules and regulations. How any British government could allow the French and Germans to destroy our beautiful apple orchards by stealth, when they could not destroy them with bombs, I will never know. The local river was clear and sported millions of fish. Today the river has been totally polluted and there is not a fish in sight because the local government allowed factories to pour out destructive toxins into the river killing all the fish. In those far-off days, there was roach, perch, and even large-size pike which occupied their own space in what the locals called the "black hole." This was a wide deep stretch of water flowing near a railway bridge. I spent many hours fishing and never caught any fish, just eels.

I was introduced to the local school which was situated a couple of miles away, just the other side of a large allotment on which the farmer grew strawberries. When they started to ripen he used to sit outside a shed, and every time a group of children crossed his patch on their way to school he would stand up waving a stick, with his dog barking nearby. Should any of us stop to tie a shoelace and grab an unsuspecting strawberry, then the farmer would roar like a mad bull and dash after us waving his stick and set the dog to chase us off the allotment.

A few miles between Abbey View and Breedon Hill was Pershore aerodrome which housed a squadron of Wellington Bombers. Every night they took off laden with bombs and skimmed the rooftops so closely that the buildings shook as they went on their raids of destruction. When they returned in the early hours of the next morning their engine note could be totally different. Some planes came back with only one engine spluttering and coughing, and made emergency landings. Others never came back and were lost over Germany.

Directly opposite where we lived were miles and miles of apple orchards where Italian prisoners of war worked. They were often seen climbing up the trees and throwing plums and apples to the children. They were a happy, laughing bunch of men who were obviously never going to attempt an escape. They were safe and sound in the depth of the British countryside, and every evening they marched back to their billets with hardly any escort.

At around nine years of age my mother bought me a brand-new bicycle from the factory where she worked in Birmingham. Then my father was called up, even though he was over forty years of age, and served in the Royal Artillery for over four years. Every person rode bicycles in the country because there were no cars, buses or trains for local journeys, and so it was cycling or walking.

My Change of Gravity

One sunny day a friend and I climbed over a fence and started walking through an apple orchard. My friend climbed high up into a tree and filled his lumber jacket with apples and tightened the lower belt to stop them falling out, then climbed down the tree. I had not started filling my pockets with apples when suddenly we heard a great bellow through the trees, as the farmer came stamping towards us carrying a large stick, with his dog bounding along by his side. My friend and I ran like the wind, dodging through the orchard. Then, right before us, barring our escape, was a great thick thorny hedge towering up into the sky at least seven feet high. The dog was furiously snapping at our heels as we hurtled towards the obstacle. I arrived first and leapt into the air with all my might. I flew up like a bird and felt as light as a feather as I rolled sideways over the top of the hedge, which was about three feet wide, and as I fell into the next field I heard the farmer laying into my friend with his stick. I ran towards the road and shot off back home. The next day I ventured back into the same orchard and stood directly in front of the gigantic thick thorny hedge. I then tried to jump high into the air, but this time I could not get my head high enough to reach the top regardless of how many times or how hard I tried. Yet the day before, I had literally leapt up and flew over that hedge like a racehorse jumping over Beecher's Brook at Aintree in the Grand National.

I did not find out why or how I managed to jump so high. Could fear and a surge of adrenalin have placed wings on my feet? Because as I lifted off, I literally floated up in to the air as though gravity did not exist, rolled over the top of the hedge and plunged down to the other side. I was always a good high-jumper even at that age, but where did I get the strength and energy to make such a massive leap? Was it just fear and adrenalin that lifted me up into the sky or was there another explanation? For a couple of seconds I seemed to transcend the physical plane, rather like the mystic Daniel Dunglass Hume who, during the Victorian era, could fly out of an upstairs window then float back again without any form of visible trickery, always in front of witnesses. Could the power of the mind-force change the gravitational response of an object and, if so, could it be that for a moment in time I had inadvertently transcended the force of gravity?

Peter Reid owned a large white Angora rabbit which he kept in a hutch outside the coal shed. Occasionally he brought it inside the house during an evening, where it used to sit still as a rock in front of the fire for hours hardly moving a muscle. One evening when we were all sitting around the fire, the lights fused and the room was plunged into darkness. Suddenly I felt a sharp pain on my kneecap, and when the lights came back on, I found teeth marks embedded in my knee, and blood running down my leg. The only culprit in the room was the rabbit. So it must have leapt at me as the lights went out and sank its teeth into my kneecap, then leapt back on to the rug in front of the fire as innocent as can be. Or could it have been another type of entity which suddenly appeared when the lights went out? Why would a docile creature suddenly launch itself at me in the dark and sink its teeth into my knee? Could there have been some sort of intelligence activating that rabbit to cause me an injury, and maybe it was not my knee it was aiming for? The subtle energies that vibrate throughout the universe can manifest in many different ways especially if the dark and destructive side of nature manifests through time and space.

The seasons changed one by one as summer turned to autumn and then winter. This ushered in sub-zero temperatures causing the local brook to freeze over, and there was snow and ice everywhere. Then another interesting event occurred. Due to my previous great leap in the apple orchard, I developed a technique in the school playground of running towards a wall, and whilst wearing rubber soled shoes, leaping into the air as high as I could and simply running up the wall by taking three or four steps. This process then elevated me to about ten feet before crashing back to earth. I was the talk of the school as the boy who could run up a wall. Once again, could this event have been the result of some superior being playing games from another dimension? During that very cold winter, I was running like the wind in the school playground then slipped and fell forward on to my knees with a powerful crash. When I stood up my right knee was bleeding profusely, and the teacher bathed it and I was sent home. A few days later my knee started to fester and became very stiff, so I was taken to Pershore hospital and, after an examination, the consultant informed me that I might have something embedded under my kneecap, and it would have to be surgically removed. During surgery they found a large sharp stone had embedded itself under my kneecap when I fell in the school playground. I spent a week in hospital because the knee was festering and gangrene could have set in, which meant that I would have needed a wooden leg and a parrot that squawked 'pieces of eight,' a la Long John Silver.

However, during that winter my leg was bandaged and as stiff as a poker, and during the ice and snow I was unable to walk from Pinvin to Pershore hospital which was situated about three miles away. So Mrs Reid sat me on the pannier above the back wheel of her bicycle and ferried me back and forth, to and from the hospital, until the knee was repaired. I thought I would never bend it again. However, about three months later I had recovered and was able to run like the wind once more. Was there a guardian angel looking after me?

When the spring and summer arrived in the Vale of Evesham, there could not have been a more beautiful place on planet earth, with the apple orchards in full blossom, the local river meandering through the countryside, mile upon mile of farmland with barns and haystacks in abundance. The country girls I found terrifying because on one occasion I went down to the river with a friend who decided to go for a swim. He took all his clothes off and waded into the river. Then a group of local girls arrived, grabbed his clothes and ran off into a nearby field. When he came out of the water, his clothes were gone. The girls came back and started prodding and tickling him. He went as red as a beetroot and ran stark naked for his life, disappearing into the distance. I shot off the other way just in case they turned their attention on to me. I never found out what happened because the next day he clammed up and never spoke about the incident. On another occasion a couple of girls approached me, giggled and said, "We found a French letter on the hedge back there." I said, "What does it say?" They screamed with laughter at my total ignorance because I had never seen or heard of such an item before.

Then as the war retreated there was no further bombing in the midlands, and I reluctantly returned back to Birmingham. Mrs Reid asked me if I was ready to return to my home in Birmingham and I remember saying that I would prefer to stay in the country, rather than go back to the city.

Chapter Five
My Return to Birmingham

On my return to Birmingham at around the age of eleven, I started my fourth school. This was situated in Golden Hillock Road, Sparkbrook; about ten minutes walk from our house. I made various friends and enemies in the school often ending up with many a fistfight in the classroom and on my way home. One great friendship with Geoffrey Franklin has lasted all our lives, and Geoffrey now lives overseas. My first sight of Geoffrey occurred when he charged at me in the school playground and gave me a right hook to the side of my head. Just as we squared up for fisticuffs, the whistle blew and all the children stopped dead in their tracks. We all lined up and were marched into our various classrooms. We sat in rows, two pupils to each desk, and my partner was a lad called Ronnie Allen. Somehow we never saw eye to eye so we fought each other in classroom, playground and after school with an ever on-going saga. There were no knives or clubs, no kicking, just fists, and if any one of us went down, the other would stand back and wait until he stood up to resume the scrap. Then we eventually gave up exhausted and went home.

After school dozens of boys marched up to the local park and played football. There was also a vast patch of ground at the back of the school which we called the allotments. Numerous factories dumped waste in this area, but there was a flat space about the size of a football pitch right behind one factory, with a small river about one hundred and fifty yards away, so we set up our game between the two obstacles and played for hours. On one occasion we set up the pitch with one goal within a few feet from the riverbank. When we attacked that area, I pulled the ball down and blasted it to one side of the goalkeeper, who leapt up and backwards so high and far that he flew over the riverbank and disappeared into the water like an Olympic diver. Fortunately, the river was quite shallow but we all howled with laughter as he staggered out dripping wet. I seemed to have a considerable ability to play football in those days, and when I reached the age of twelve, I was selected for the school football team, playing inside right. We never lost a game whilst I was playing and won the South Birmingham Schools League Championship. Then next year half the team left, including all the best players, then they made me captain, playing left half. Ronnie Allen was also in the team and we still ended up with arguments and fisticuffs. Geoffrey had by then moved on to a local Art College and later made it to The Royal College of Art in London. He then taught art in Taunton before retiring from teaching and moving to the Far East, and recently he has obtained a Doctorate. Not many youngsters from the Birmingham area that I grew up in made it to a university because Oxford or Cambridge to my generation was about the same distance as the Moon. So when I eventually arrived in Oxford, it was on a bicycle riding with the Solihull cycling club on a training run. I think it was Spike Milligan who said on a TV interview that he went to Oxford, and when the interviewer asked him what was he doing there, Spike replied in his goon show voice, "Buying a Tie."

During our summer holidays, myself, Geoffrey, and another boy called Basil, collected comics such as the Beano and Wizard. In a nearby district called Balsall Heath we found a dark dingy shop which looked as though it had dropped right out of the last century. It was a shop specializing in selling and buying comics. The owner was the most disreputable character we had ever seen, and he was the spitting image of the Dickens character Fagin, portrayed in Oliver Twist. He stooped low and rubbed his hands, his fingernails were long and dirty, and he was unshaven with grimy stubble on his chin. His jacket was torn and his baggy trousers looked far too big for his thin frame, and his shoes were almost falling off his feet with a flapping sole on his right foot. "Hello Boys," he would say in his broad Black Country accent, washing his hands even faster and crouching down with his elbows high in the air, like the wings of a giant bluebottle. "What are you looking for," he would say, and then occasionally he would depart into the back of the shop and return; one day with a 1932 Wizard, which he displayed with great gusto. "Worth a lot of money," he said proudly. He looked very much like a giant bluebottle, hardly ever washed and stank like a turd, so we called him Turdy Bottlewash.

The summer months in the late 1940's was spent riding bicycles every evening and during the school holidays, Geoffrey, Basil and I formed a trio. Many evenings we rode out to Earlswood Lakes which were situated about seven miles from Sparkbrook. Within minutes we were in the country lanes of Warwickshire, and fifteen minutes later we reached our destination before returning at dusk as we raced furiously back home. I was very slim and slender, Geoffrey was rippling with huge muscles and Basil was even more massive. Both could leave me standing in a sprint but I could keep on pounding away, not giving them much chance to regain their breath after a furious sprint, which occurred whenever we passed a thirty miles per hour road sign.

Basil's Rejuvenating Machine

Later in life Basil became notorious, with his escapades reported in the Times Newspaper. Due to the fact that he trained as an auto electrical engineer, he started to invent various electrical gadgets, one of which landed him in hot water in the USA with the FBI fingering his collar. According to the Times, he invented an electrical black box which he claimed would improve health and increase longevity, so he went to the USA and organized a series of lectures in top hotels, in order to sell his product to ageing Americans. It appears that he was quite successful at first, and then the penny dropped because after plugging his electric box into the mains, the other side was connected to a narrow probe, which emitted a low electrical pulse. Then he persuaded geriatric Americans to stick the probe up their bums and turn on the power. He swore that the energy would reduce ageing and promote health. He managed to get thousands of aged American citizens purchasing his product. Eventually the FBI accosted him after a few people complained that it did not work.

My First Job

When I was fourteen years of age I left school and started work in a photographic processing lab. This turned out to be something like the "Goon Show." I went for an interview with my father and was offered my first job. The managing director was a bald rotund porker of a man sitting behind a large desk. He looked me up and down over the rim of his glasses and said. "I will take you on next Monday at twenty-eight shillings per week" which today is the equivalent of £1.40. I was informed that I would need a cow gown, this being a light brown coat used to avoid splashing developer and chemicals on to my regular clothing. Then at eight-thirty on the last day of 1946, I presented myself at the office, slotted my card into a machine that recorded my time of arrival. Once inside the building I perceived a vast emporium, it was about half the size of a football pitch, with a wide staircase at the far end leading up to a surrounding balcony. At the top of the stairs was a designated area for tea and lunch breaks complete with tables and bench seats. Behind the staircase on the ground floor was a dark passageway, leading to numerous dark rooms. Just to the right was a vast room illuminated by a light green safelight with ten manned contact printing machines pounding away non-stop all day. Each person sat at a desk which incorporated a light box. Before the films were cut into strips, each negative was graded by pressing a knee pad, which lit up the box, showing a needle indicating density and contrast. One of three different grades of paper was selected, matching the contrast and density of the negative, and then each print was stamped with a number after which they were thrown into a massive bath of developer. Another operator watched the images appearing before moving each print into a fixing bath for ten minutes. Great batches of prints were then transferred into one of three revolving washing baths which was cascading and swirling around to finally wash the prints before glazing. During the summer season, around twenty thousand pictures were individually printed every day. Outside in the light, there were six large revolving glazing machines each about three feet in diameter.

My first job was to remove the washed prints from the bowls, place them in lines on a taut cloth that continuously revolved around the drum. As they fell off at the other end, rows of girls gathered up the prints, matching them with film numbers which were stamped on the back of each print. Then they were placed in special envelopes for despatch to dealers and chemists all over the midlands. I spent my days running up and down the production line servicing those continuously moving machines. After three months, I was promoted to the film-developing darkroom which was situated on the right side of the building. Written on the wall outside the doorway were the words:
"All ye who enter here abandon hope"
On entering the outer doorway covered with a dark curtain I perceived a passageway about ten yards long painted jet black, so no light could reflect back into the actual darkroom, that also had a heavy dark curtain covering the holy place. The darkroom was

illuminated by a green safelight, and this was so dark, that it took about half-an-hour for my eyes to become acclimatised in order to see what was there. It was very spooky working in such dark conditions and often I felt the presence of the other dimension when working in such low-level illumination. The room was about thirty feet long with about eight developing, rinsing, fixing and finally washing tanks. They were about four feet deep by two feet wide and set into the floor. At one end of the room was a pile of boxes on a table, each containing thirty films in separate compartments with a top clip about five inches long containing a ticket to coincide with each undeveloped film. Two boys worked in this film developing room, and after unrolling each film, they attached a weighted clip to one end letting the film unroll, then the top clip was attached and placed on a metal rack, with thirty hooks matching the number of films per box. Then every five minutes, an electronic motor would lift up a pair of long girders the length of the room, and after attaching to the rack of films, it was lowered into the first developing tank. When the racks of film reached the other end of the darkroom they were washed and individually placed in a light-proof cupboard, which was opened from the outside. Finally, the developed films were slotted into a drying cabinet before being transferred into the printing room.

The Crazy Characters

The place was full of crazy characters, starting with the porker-like MD, who during the busy summer season ran up and down outside the darkroom screaming - "More Boxes," which meant that we were urged to work faster so that they could be re-filled with more films, which kept the production line going full-tilt. We had a one-eyed foreman, with a patch over his left eye, whose favourite saying was, "One eye, one arm, and one arsehole," before bursting into laughter as he hustled the workforce into action. Up in the gallery was the workshop containing a character called Harry, who was responsible for maintenance. He had the most pronounced Black Country accent imaginable, and when I was instructed to give him a hand I remember him shouting; "Shut That Doer" as I entered his province. The word *door* was pronounced differently in the Black Country.

I often wondered whether comedian Larry Grayson, who years later used the same catch-phrase had heard Harry yelling those words, or was it a coincidence. Jung called it synchronicity, when two or more events happened of a similar nature, whilst they were totally unconnected in the material world. Harry was about five feet tall and stooped low as he walked, with his feet splayed outwards at an angle of about forty-five degrees. His head rolled from side to side, and he had a hatchet-shaped face, a receding chin, and protruding teeth. In fact he was the nearest thing to a human rodent that I had ever seen. On one occasion when the work dried up in mid-winter, I was assigned the task of helping the dear man. His workshop was like going back in time to Victorian days, with tools of every type lining the dirty greasy walls. The floor had never been swept for years, and engine parts were piled up in every corner. When he was called down to the floor below by the MD to check a specific machine I found a door at the back of his workshop which led directly on to the roof. I walked out and before me was a flat roof with a flagpole at the front of the building, so I climbed up the pole. I used to do stupid things like that when I was a boy. Then Harry appeared through the open doorway, looked right and left, but did not look up. Then with a screech he rushed to the edge of the building and peered over the rim. I let out a laugh which gave him the shock of his life. He then jumped in to the air, raised his head and screamed in his broad Black Country accent, "Yow nerly gave me art attack."

There were about fifty staff all told and most of them were either boys of my own age or local girls, plus a few male adults in their mid-forties. The men were paid about £4.50 per week, the girls £2.50, and the boys from £1.40 to £2 per week. Today those figures seem unbelievable. However, my father earning about £5 per week was able to rent our three bedroom family house, for fifty pence per week, including rates. We now live in a totally different world!

The Staff

There was one girl they called "Ding Dong Doris," and when in my innocence, I asked why she so called, I was informed that if she ever got me in to the darkroom on my own I would undoubtedly hear bells ringing. Then there was "Bicycle Betty," so named because she often gave the foreman a ride in the darkroom. "Blodwyn Blanket" came from that foreign country west of Hereford, and was so named because she encouraged some of the older boys to stretch out on top of her in one of the darkrooms. The MD's name was Mr. Dik, and four of his sons worked in the business, so there was a quite surplus of Diks in the factory. During 1947, blizzards raged for over two months with snowdrifts piled up on every pavement, so it was very difficult to get to and from work. However, the main roads were kept clear by snowploughs and gritting lorries working all through the night. When the snow eventually departed then that glorious summer of 1947 came alive. Every lunch-time the staff flocked out into the street to keep cool in whatever shade was available. There was a car and bicycle park next to the factory, with an old hunchback in charge.

On one occasion a woman, probably in her seventies, had an argument with the said gentleman, and then swung a right hook to his jaw, which knocked him off his feet. Another elderly woman arrived and screamed, "What did yow do that for," in her Black Country accent, then slapped her face. Next minute both women squared up to each other, like a pair of boxers in a ring and started throwing punches with wild swinging fists. Within a few minutes hundreds of people came pouring out of different factories and formed a ring of spectators to witness the fight. After about five minutes punching and scratching, with blood splattering down their faces, and the crowd roaring them on, one woman landed a powerful blow sending the other one flat on her back. So ended the fight.

Change of Job

After two years, I was offered another job with a firm specialising in industrial photography. Here I learned how to hand-print quality pictures from 10x8 sizes up to six feet wide. I worked with a chief printer who looked like a pantomime wizard, with long white hair brushed back over his balding forehead. He had a long pointed twitching nose, long thin fingers, and long fingernails. When he was shading a negative, in order to either lighten or darken an area during printing, he waved his long fingers in a circular motion, flicking them in and out of the projected light beam, as though he was casting a spell. Occasionally a small mouse would appear on one of the enlargers and run down the electric cable to safety when we arrived in the morning. When a giant enlargement of around six feet or more was needed for industrial exhibitions, we had to wait until it was dark then transfer a huge roll of bromide paper from the darkroom through the main sorting room, which had a glass roof, then into the studio at the far end. After switching on a green safelight, we set up the studio camera complete with a large size negative and darkroom enlarging light which was projected horizontally on to the opposite wall. When it was focussed and the lens stopped down, we unrolled a giant size piece of paper and stuck it to the wall at the far end of the studio. Then an exposure was made, this could be around thirty seconds or more, depending on the density of the negative. After which the exposed print was rolled up and transported back to the darkroom for developing. Today I look back in amazement at the antics that followed in order to develop the giant pictures. There was a shallow sink about nine feet long set into the floor against a plain dark wall. The giant print was unrolled and stuck on the wall and then it was washed with cold water from a hosepipe. Two buckets of warm developer was placed either side containing a great mass of cotton wool. When the chief printer screamed, "Go," we grabbed a handful of well-soaked cotton wool then covered the whole picture area from top to bottom, until it was covered with developer. When the image started to appear, the chief printer dashed about with a combination of hot water and neat developer, to bring out certain areas of the picture until it was finally developed. It was then hosed down with cold water, rolled up and dunked into a large fixing bath. After fixing, it was washed for half an hour, then hung up to dry outside in the main building. After a total of four years darkroom work, at the age of eighteen years, I was conscripted into the Royal Air Force for two years National Service as an RAF Policeman.

Two Years National Service

At the recruiting office, I was persuaded to sign on as a regular for three years, instead of the standard two years national service, but after attending Cardington camp in the middle of winter I refused to sign the final document. There was nothing that they could do legally so I returned home to Birmingham and waited for my final call up papers, ordering me to the RAF National Service Training Camp at Padgate. This was a demand that by law I could not refuse, so I presented myself with a group of other lads around the same age, and started my national service with what is called square-bashing. Up in the morning in sub-zero temperatures, making up your bed to exact dimensions, polishing boots and buttons until they shone like mirrors, then walking across a quadrangle to the wash-house to shave in freezing cold water. Breakfast was served at 0800 hrs, after which we were lined up for a billet inspection where every item of kit had to be placed according to a diagram pinned to the wall. The floor had to be highly polished, and cloth pads were used to walk on in order to keep the floor spotless. A large drill instructor entered the room and we all leapt to attention while he inspected every bed, area of floor, and each uniform for the slightest defect. Then we grabbed our rifles and lined up outside the billet and were marched on to the parade ground. We stood to attention, shouldered arms, then marched around for hours on end until it was time for lunch when we were marched back to our billet, and on to the cookhouse. We were marched on to the rifle range and instructed in the art of firing a rifle at circular targets almost like a dartboard. Physical fitness instructors took us for long runs, and ferocious exercises in between rifle drills. If I remember correctly, it took eight weeks of murderous slog before we were passed out fit for action. After the initial training, I was drafted into the RAF police and then posted to Pershore, Worcestershire, for my initial police training, where I was evacuated during the war years.

RAF Police Training

This was an extension of the original square bashing, except that it was much more intensified and the pressure was vast. We also studied law, and had to take three examinations before passing out.

We were taught Judo and self-defence, and the use of many weapons including Bren guns, Rifles, Sten guns and Pistols. We went on murderous long-distance runs and we were given ferocious exercises. Eventually we passed out as acting corporals, and we were issued with the regulation white caps and webbing, hence the nickname 'Snowdrops'. A number of the group was selected for an advanced driving course at Netheravon in Wiltshire, including myself. After presenting myself at the camp, square-bashing ceased to exist during the eight weeks duration of the driving course. We were not allowed to wear boots, only rubber-soled trainers.

We started by driving a fifteen-hundredweight truck around the runways of the airfield, with no other vehicle in sight, so we could make all the mistakes imaginable. There were about eight of us in the back of a truck, and then we took it in turns to drive the brute. There were no side windows, no heating, and no modern synchromesh gear box so we had to learn on a crash gearbox. This meant that when you wanted to change gear, you pressed the clutch down to the floor, moved the gear stick into neutral, removed your foot from the clutch, and then revved up the engine until it obtained the correct revs. You then slammed the clutch back to the floor, slotted the gear into second and only then, let out the clutch. If you got the revs wrong, you could not change gear and the truck rolled along in neutral, so then you lost control.

Once we got the hang of this system it was easy, but how many drivers today can use a crash gearbox with safety. Also at Netheravon was situated the police dog school, and believe me, they were not normal dogs because some creatures were the spitting image of long legged timber wolves. Most of the dog handlers were bitten a few times by one of the ferocious beasts before they graduated.

On one occasion I was standing outside the guardroom when in the distance I saw two huge wolfine creatures loping towards me. The policeman on duty grabbed my arm and dragged me into the safety of the guardroom as they loped past snarling and growling. Then all hell was let loose because they were trained killers, and could not be let loose on the local population. So truckloads of police and dog handlers shot out with nets and loaded weapons and eventually located and cornered the beasts. After months of drill and discipline, it was heaven to be allowed such freedom during the eight-week course. We were also informed that the course would include a civilian driving license as well as the RAF document. During the last week we were all tested individually in the fifteen-hundredweight truck by driving on the roads outside the camp. One day when driving down a small deserted lane with a high bank either side, suddenly a huge tank appeared to my left, towered above the truck, then rolled down the bank and climbed up the other side and disappeared from view. It was a very close encounter because we had strayed on to a tank range without realizing the danger. When it was my turn to take the driving test, I set out towards Salisbury. As we entered the town, I drove along a narrow street, and in front of me was a woman crossing the road. Because I was only doing around twenty miles per hour, I assessed that she would be well on to the footpath by the time I reached her crossing, so I did not brake. The examiner looked across and said. "Did you not see that woman crossing the road?" I replied, "I would have missed her by a mile at the speed I was travelling." Then he instructed me to stop when we were driving up a massive incline. I stopped, put the hand brake on, and then revved up the engine and as I let the clutch out, the vehicle rolled backwards which meant that I had failed my test. With nothing to lose, I decided to show the examiner how well I could handle the vehicle at speed, so I revved up, slammed through the gears without a fault, hurtled around a few corners at forty miles per hour and zoomed back to the camp like a rocket, as fast as the truck would go. I shot through the camp gates and stamped on my brakes, switched off the engine and waited for the verdict. "You have passed," he said, "Take it away." I nearly fell out of the cab with shock, and thought. "My God, now I will have to drive one of these trucks by myself."

Advanced Training

I was then posted back to Pershore for an advanced provost-training course, which was a more intensified version of the two initial training courses, and further law studies. Next I was accosted by an army major running a commando course at Oxford, so I volunteered to learn their nasty techniques of how to kill people. On the first day, the major gathered a group around him then produced a hand grenade, pulled out the pin, handed the live grenade to me and said, "You have exactly ten seconds to throw that bomb before it blows you up." I hurled it as far as I could, and we all hit the ground as it exploded in the distance. "In this game you have to think very quickly to survive," he said. Next he produced a tin hat, shoved a stick of explosives into the ground, placed the tin hat on top and lit the fuse. We all jumped back. Then, when the explosion occurred the tin hat disappeared into the sky. Next he produced a flat object which was a small explosive device, and then buried it in the ground. This object will not explode when you tread on it, but as soon as you stride forward taking your foot off the plate it will go bang right between your legs. We call this weapon a "De-bollocker" for obvious reasons. During the next few weeks we crawled through tunnels and under barbed wire while live bullets were pinging above our heads; we climbed though trenches filled with water, swarmed up and down ropes, and fired all kinds of weapons. We fought each other with hand-to-hand combat, and we were shown how and where to knife, or shoot the enemy for maximum effect. On returning to Pershore, I was interviewed by the station commander and sent to Whitehall in London for an interview with the Provost Marshall for a possible job in the Special Investigation Branch of the RAF police. I knew that I was too young and inexperienced for such a position, and sure enough, I was not offered the job. Then I was posted to Bishop Briggs in Scotland.

The RAF and a squadron of American Thunder Jet pilots, flying out from Renfrew airport which is now Glasgow airport, inhabited the camp. Our job was to patrol the airfield with dog handlers, especially during the hours of darkness. We were issued with Smith & Wesson revolvers, and six rounds of ammo. I was there for only ten days before being posted to Hucknall near Nottingham. Before leaving Glasgow, I was accosted by the American base commander enquiring why so many items had gone missing from the American Stores. We RAF police looked after the main guardroom and had access to every key on the base, so he assumed it was one of us that had pilfered the stores. So I started an investigation to find out who was on duty when the items went missing. Sure enough one of our corporals was on duty every time security was breached. We searched his locker and found most of the missing items. He was charged, court marshalled, reduced to the ranks and sent to Colchester. Believe it or not his name was Corporal Fiddler. With a name like that you would have thought that he should have kept to the straight and narrow. After spending nine months training, I was at last posted to a permanent camp at Hucknell near Nottingham.

On arrival I was asked to take a truck to a specific airfield and pick up some engineering materials. I was also asked to take a passenger who was with the Canadian Air Force, so we set out and belted down to the location on the south coast. After loading up the gear we started back to Hucknell, and the Canadian asked whether he could have a drive, so I pulled up and gave him the wheel. When he started the engine it was obvious that he had never driven a vehicle with a crash gearbox because he grated the gears with every change. When we approached an island, and he managed to ram the gears into neutral, then as we roared into the bend at about forty miles per hour, he just about managed to keep the vehicle on the road as it swerved around the bend then hit the curb on the other side of the island, bounced up into the air like a kangaroo, and shot across the pavement behind a bus shelter - then bounced back on to the road. Fortunately the shelter was empty and no one was hurt. I screamed for him to stamp on the brakes, and when we eventually came to a stop, I resumed my seat behind the wheel, and asked him where he learnt to drive, also what type of license he possessed. He replied, "I do not have a license. This is my first lesson." I could have been court marshalled if there had been an accident. I just assumed that he had a license; otherwise he would not have asked me to let him drive.

Our job at Hucknell was to patrol Nottingham, Derby, Leicester, Peterborough and Loughborough, using many different types of vehicles from the usual fifteen-hundredweight trucks, Land Rovers, Standard Vanguard saloons, and Hillman saloons. We set off in teams of four, and fingered a few collars, mainly for incorrect dress. We then all congregated at the NAFFI club in Nottingham at midnight, before racing back over the golf course road to see who could get back to camp in the shortest possible time.

Every so often the RAF would organize an escape and evasion exercise. One hundred aircrew all wearing blue denim were dropped in one county, such as Leicestershire. They had to get over the border into the next county without being apprehended during a forty-eight hour period. Our job was to seek out and detain the enemy at all costs. We parked vehicles at strategic places all over the county. The first night I was on patrol with a man called Burt Banner, who in civilian life was a farmer in Warwickshire. We parked our vehicle in the dead of night in a deserted gateway near a wood, and then Burt said that he heard someone coughing in the field opposite. We climbed over the gateway in pitch darkness then slowly made our way across the field. Suddenly Burt whispered, "Hold down this wire, while I climb over and see who is there." I found the wire and pressed it down, and then I leapt into the air with shock because it was an electrified fence. Being a farmer he knew all along that the ping, ping, ping that we heard was the electricity passing through the wire fence, and it was cows in the field that were coughing, not aircrew.

We were given a pack of food and drink to tide us over the night vigil, and then as dawn approached, we spotted a definite suspect creeping along the side of the hedge, so we called to arms and leapt over the fence in pursuit. The figure was very fast, and jumped over a hedge into an adjacent wood. We followed the sound of a crashing body for a few minutes, and then all was silent. We stood completely still and listened but were unable to detect the slightest sound. After about fifteen minutes searching, we gave up the chase and sat on a fallen tree trunk. Suddenly we heard the sound of a hunting horn being blown. "Bugger me," Burt blurted out. "The Bloody Vikings are coming." Then we heard a massive crashing in the bushes, as though a giant creature was forcing its way through the trees. Suddenly a huge horse appeared with a fellow in a red coat seated in the saddle. "Have you seen a fox passing this way?" he said, "No" we replied, so he turned tail and loped off back where he came from. Towards the end of the exercise we had apprehended at least half of the aircrew. However, the next morning, as dawn was breaking, I was sitting in the back of a civilian Jaguar police car, proceeding in a convoy of about ten vehicles, and suddenly they all stopped because in a large field about two hundred yards away was a skulking, creeping figure. About twenty civilian and RAF police combined hurtled out of their vehicles to apprehend the slouching figure. A policeman sitting on my left in the back of the car opened his door and leapt out to do battle, and then as I leaned forward to get out on his side he inadvertently slammed the door on my head. I fell back, half unconscious, seeing stars everywhere and ended up with a large bump on my head.

When I started to focus, I perceived the so-called enemy figure running like hell back to his farmhouse, pursued by a dozen screaming policemen. Then he hauled out a shotgun to defend himself because the poor farmer had no idea why so many lunatics were screaming for his blood. Eventually we calmed him down by explaining the reason for our blood lust. Once the exercise ended we all trooped back to camp and made our report. Not many of the aircrew managed to cross the border, but some did evade our security

Banned From Driving
I was eventually banned from driving. On one escape and evasion exercise when driving a Hillman Hunter vehicle, I parked on the grass

verge in order to check a nearby field, and the wheels were stuck firmly in the muddy ground, so I could not extract the vehicle from mother earth. Unfortunately, the Wing Commander in charge of the operation suddenly appeared directly in front of the car shouting for me to get a move on. I furiously revved up the engine and let out the clutch a bit too fiercely, so the car bounced up in the air and shot forward at a frantic pace. The Wing Commander was near the front of the car and had to jump for his life, landing head-first in the wet muddy ditch. When he re-appeared covered with mud, he was red in the face and foaming at the mouth, so I shot off down the road in double quick time, leaving him dancing with rage. Naturally he organized an investigation and I was banned from driving and transferred to another camp, which was Bridgenorth in Shropshire. I never drove another vehicle in the RAF. I was assigned to guardroom duty and all outside patrols ceased for the remainder of my national service. On arriving at Bridgenorth I was billeted in the main guardroom complex. My duties consisted of looking after the guardroom on a rotor basis. Eight hours on duty, then sixteen hours off, with an occasional weekend free during which time I cycled the twenty-six miles to Birmingham and back again.

Riding Shotgun

It was basically a dull job in comparison to the evening patrols in my previous camp. However, because it was a basic training camp for recruits, the RAF police were responsible for collecting the camp's wages every Thursday from a Bridgenorth bank. On the appointed hour a vehicle would arrive outside the guardroom complete with driver, accounts clerk, and a senior officer. I would then open up the pistol cupboard and produce a Smith & Wesson revolver with six rounds of ammunition, complete with gun holster, then ride shotgun down into the middle of the town like John Wayne in one of the old Western Films. We stopped near a side entrance of the bank while I stood guard with my hand on the six shooter then the team dashed up the entry, collected the loot, threw the sacks of money into the boot then we high-tailed it back to camp. There was never any attempt to bushwack the vehicle whilst I was at the camp. Whether it ever happened after I left the RAF I have no idea, but with an armed guard, the average crook would probably never attempt to rob the Royal Air Force.

A Very Serious Charge

I was on duty one night when a drill instructor arrived in the guardroom with a recruit in tow. "Charge this airman with attempted murder," he screamed. "He tried to brain me from behind with an iron bar." We charged him and sent for the medical officer to check his physical and mental state.

The recruit was a small Scottish man from Glasgow, who swore at every person, then threatened that he would send for his razor gang from Glasgow who would carve all of us up into pieces. The guardroom was situated with a quadrangle in the centre of the building, which was used to exercise prisoners. One afternoon, the razor boy somehow broke loose and found a hatchet in a cupboard, then proceeded to scream like a banshee chasing two big six-foot policemen into the main building. They slammed the door shut and left him in the open. Then he ran around, smashing the hatchet against doors and windows, screaming that he was going to kill us all - until eventually it started to rain. When he was soaking wet, he gave up the chase and surrendered. We shut him back in his cell, and later he was court marshalled and sent to Colchester.

Two weeks later they sent him back saying that they could do nothing with him. By now the station commander was undecided what to do, so I suggested that the Glasgow razor boy should be discharged forthwith from the RAF. The station commander instantly agreed. As he strode through the gates for the last time, he bellowed, "When I get back to Glasgow, I am going to bring my razor gang down here and carve you into bits and pieces." Fortunately we never heard from him again. I spent the last nine months of my national service at Bridgenorth and was much relieved when I too was discharged from the RAF, and returned to my previous civilian life in professional photography.

Chapter Six
Astral Vision

During my early teen years, whilst working as a photographic printer, I started playing cricket, table tennis and football, and I was also involved with cycling. Later I joined the Solihull cycling club and rode in a few races. However, just before I left school, a very strange event occurred during a cricket match. I was never a very good batsman or bowler, but when I went into bat, my eyesight started to fail. All I could see was spots before my eyes, like being caught in a great snowstorm. When I took up my position in front of the wicket, I could only see a faint outline of the bowler at the other end of the crease, and all detail had disappeared. Then I saw an outline of his raised arm and assumed that he was in the process of delivering a fast ball, so I strode forward and swung my bat without setting eyes on the ball. There was a sharp crack as I swiped the ball for a six. The next ball I also struck with great precision, even though I could not see the missile. I continued to play by instinct, managing to knock up fifty runs without ever seeing the ball. I can't remember the overall score, but later, when my sight returned, I was never able to knock up fifty runs in any match again. When we were fielding my sight was even worse, with the complete landscape and players hardly visible, as through I was looking through a blinding snowstorm.

It was in reality a bright sunny day with not a cloud in the sky, and I was situated near the boundary but could not see anything through the great snowy mist that blighted my eyesight. I could only make out shapes in the distance. As the blurred figure of the batsman strode forward and swung his bat, I heard the sound of a ball crashing against willow. I turned and ran with my arm outstretched and suddenly, without a glimpse of the ball, it dropped in to the palm of my hand like magic. There was applause all round for my great catch. Believe it or not, the complete episode was again repeated when I made a second great catch without ever having sight of the ball. At that age, I had no idea of the implications of the day's events, and after the match I managed to find my bicycle and rode home, even though I could not see the road in front of me. When I arrived home I went straight up to my room and went to bed without telling my parents what had happened. The next morning when I woke up, my sight was restored to normal, and I did not mention the day's events to a living soul. Without a shadow of doubt, something very unusual was in operation that day, transcending the known laws of the universe.

"How could anyone score fifty runs, and make two impossible catches without actually seeing the ball."
It was years later that I managed to gain insight into the "Multi Dimensional Universe," and the powerful energy that circulated through every atom of creation.

The Power of the Mind Force

Another interesting event took place at a later date. One day I was bent up with a terrible pain in the right side of my stomach. When the doctor arrived I was despatched straight to hospital, and appendicitis was diagnosed. I did not like the idea of being carved up, so next morning when they came to examine me; I informed the doctor that the pain had gone. This was a complete lie, and a very dangerous thing to do because I could have developed peritonitis. When they poked and prodded me, I just smiled and gritted my teeth at the pain. I was discharged and sent home. I went straight to bed and focused my mind on removing the pain and when I woke up next morning, the pain had completely disappeared. I had no idea of how I had removed the pain overnight until years later. It never occurred to me that, if a person was determined and bloody minded enough, by focusing the power of the sub-conscious mind, the course of events could be changed to such a degree in a short space of time.

A Cone of Power

During that period in my life I had never heard about the chakras, or the healing power that could be activated by the power of the mind-force. I seemed to possess much more talent for football than cricket so the next strange event occurred on a football pitch as dusk was approaching. This event I found was impossible to repeat on a regular basis and happened about once every six months, usually lasting for no more than half-an-hour during a game. Suddenly I found myself hurtling around the pitch at great speed but with hardly any effort, and my breathing was no different from when I was walking, yet I was sprinting at top speed. Then I perceived a player coming towards me to make a tackle, in what appeared to be slow motion. At the same time I could see his arms pumping furiously, fists clenched and muscles rippling on his thighs. I was aware of the ferocious expression on his face as he growled and gnashed his teeth, yet he seemed to be charging at me as though I was watching a slow motion film. At the same time, I could see where every player was on the pitch as though I was looking down from above. As my opponent stretched out a leg to make the tackle, I waited until the last second. Then as his foot appeared to be about an inch from contact, I pushed the ball sideways and jumped out of the way. He then continued his dash, still in slow motion, right past me, so I strolled down the pitch, dodging one way then the other, walked the ball past every opponent including the goal keeper, and into the net for a goal.

It was many years later that I experienced a similar event. Even though I was a reasonably good footballer, for the love of me, I could not repeat that sublime moment very often. Later in life when it happened again, I often sat down and analysed the situation because whenever such an event occurred, it seemed to me that time, in close proximity to my physical body, was operating at a different level to time outside my cone of power. How will the scientific establishment answer the question regarding the difference between the time differential inside the circle close to my body, and time on the outside? It appeared that time was not constant and could be manipulated if the conditions were right. But what were the conditions that caused a change in time, plus the high-angle vision, as though I was fifty yards up in the air observing the game from above, while my physical body was still running on the ground?

Possible Shape Shifting

Years later, I was sitting on a bench close to a football pitch with my back to the tumulus, or as we call it, Boadicea's burial ground on Hampstead Heath, London, whilst writing a few notes for an article, when two very peculiar events took place. I was so engrossed in my work that, when I stretched and looked up, hopping towards me on my left was a great big toad. It was absolutely huge, and never having seen such a creature on the Heath before, I was intrigued to find out where it had come from. It turned its head, stared at me, then hopped under my seat and disappeared, so I carried on writing. Suddenly, I felt a presence nearby, and when I looked up, sitting next to me was a huge fat man. I never heard him approach and sit down. He just appeared as if by magic, looking very much like a human version of the toad that disappeared under my bench. He did not say a word, so I carried on writing, and when I looked up a few minutes later, he too had disappeared. We have all heard of Were Wolves, so could there be such a creature as a Were Toad.? After all, if life has changed and developed over millions of years to such a level as Darwin suggested, what happens if time and space can be compressed or elongated, so that physical development could be changed in record time instead of millions of years? Could this be the answer to the legends of shape-shifters? Perhaps there may be creatures on this planet that can compress time and space so that a shape change could be organized in a matter of minutes, instead of millions of years, and then retard the process in order to return to their previous physical shape.

Whilst sitting on the same bench at a later date, a white haired man approached and sat down just as I was sharpening my pencil. The wind blew cuttings on to his lap. I looked up and apologized. He asked me what I was writing. I informed him that I believed I knew how George Best, or any other great footballer, could at times control a football with such precision, timing and balance. The man sitting next to me stated that he was just off to the University of California to lecture on the metaphysical world and was most interested in my theory. We conversed for a couple of hours and when I asked his name, I nearly fell off my seat. It was Lancelot Law White, a very well known writer and lecturer on the metaphysical world. We exchanged addresses and agreed to meet at a later date. About twelve months later, I was attending a funeral service at Golders Green crematorium and on looking at flowers laid outside the chapel of rest, L. L. White was also on the permanent guest list, so I never managed to meet up with him again to continue our conversation about why time appeared to be slower outside a cone of power, than the area inside it's perimeter. I have also witnessed many great players from the past, performing with the same magical touch, week in week out Aston Villa once had a centre forward, as they were called in the past, named George Edwards, who had the same gift as George Best. In those days there was no TV to elevate the old masters of football; so many names disappeared into oblivion. When George Edwards went on a run towards the opposite goal, he was almost unstoppable, and scored more than forty goals in one season. He had a great loping stride and a body swerve that I have never seen equalled. He seemed to sway so far to left, and then right, before turning the other way as he rounded opponent after opponent, before slotting the ball into the net. He was undoubtedly one of the great ball players, yet he is unheard of by present day supporters.

Occasionally I seemed to erect a cone of power unconsciously around myself so that time inside the cone was operating in a different dimension to time on the outside. Everything outside the cone seemed to be moving in slow motion, whilst inside the cone I had all the time in the world to move the football anyway I chose without anyone being able to get at it. This enabled me to avoid the most ferocious tackles with ease. The only trouble was it only happened once in a blue moon. Also, I recalled a game that we used to play in the school playground when I was thirteen years of age. The class stood in a circle around the playground with about eight boys in the centre. The boys outside the circle then hurled a tennis ball at the group inside the circle with the object of hitting each one in turn. They then joined the others attempting to eliminate the remaining boys inside the circle. This interesting game nearly always left me on my own after all the other boys had been eliminated because I seemed to have some strange ability to swerve at the last moment, somehow avoiding the ball, even when it was hurled at very close quarters. Once again time seemed to operate at a different level within my circle of energy, enabling me to twist and turn at the last moment, in order to avoid being struck by the ball. Many great legendary warriors of old may have developed their amazing ability to survive a battle by tuning in to this very same area of changing time within their own cone of power, whilst opponents were operating outside the time zone. If you have never experienced this amazing phenomenon, you will probably think, just like scientists and academics, that it was some form of hallucination or imagination. Is astral vision and astral travel a figment of the imagination, or a problem with the electrical or chemical area of the brain? Most scientists and medical doctors dismiss the fact that a spirit can sometimes leave the body after a great shock occurs. We all know that at death, the electrical force field ceases to exist leaving only a physical shadow of the person that once walked the earth. There have been many incidents of near death experiences where a person was involved in an accident or suffered a severe shock, or lay unconscious in a dentist's chair or hospital theatre whilst having an operation, and witnessed the proceedings as though they were looking at a TV screen. Many of these events have been proved beyond all shadow of doubt. Yet the unbelievers still insist that it was imagination or hallucination. The old saying, that proof of the pudding is in the eating, has never been truer than in these cases. No person can ever find the truth through hearsay, since you must experience the phenomena yourself before you are capable of believing. I have spent my life with one leg in the physical plane and the other in the astral plane, so I personally have no doubt whatsoever as to the validity of astral vision, astral travel, and the time differential when these events occur. After experiencing many out-of-body events in my early years, I decided to carry out a few experiments to find out whether I could astral travel at will, and set about evolving a system as follows.

My System for Astral Travel

When sitting on Hampstead Heath, London, I often watched crows circling high up in the trees, and tried to visualise exactly what they could see, and then attempt to transfer my consciousness into a crow visualizing the world through their eyes. This system starts the subconscious mind working. Then at night I lay in bed on my back and started concentrating on my physical body by relaxing my toes and feet, and after a few minutes slowly working my way up the body, concentrating on calves, thighs, hips, stomach, back, arms, hands and finally neck and facial muscles. It is surprising how tense you are until you concentrate on each individual area of your body. It usually takes about half an hour to completely relax the whole muscular system. One night, after following the above procedure while still awake, I was in a marvellous relaxed state, and then suddenly I felt a sensation as though I was in a lift hurtling downwards but at the same time I was actually rising up into the air until my face was up against the ceiling. I felt so excited that I had floated out of the body whilst remaining completely conscious. Then I turned over and received the shock of my life because, there down below me, was the body from which I had just departed. Through sheer excitement of what I had accomplished, I shot back into my physical body and woke up next day, none the worse from my experience. Later, I found that I could slip out of the body, by relaxing every muscle, though it took at least half an hour or more to get a result.

My Childhood Adventures on the Astral Plane

When I was a child, I travelled out of the body almost every night, and many times I found myself in a strange house walking along a passageway, then peering into a lounge or kitchen before slowly climbing the stairs and looking around the bedrooms watching people fast asleep in their beds. It was so real and detailed that I often wondered whether I was breaking and entering other people's houses without realising how I arrived there in the first place. Yet I always woke up next morning in my own bed. There were times when I found myself in a strange country and could not read the language that was written over shops, and at times, I saw large strange black motorcars passing up and down the roads. Often I found myself flying high in the air over mountains with lights twinkling from towns and villages miles below as I flew about the night sky.

Time Travelling

On one occasion when I was out of the body I found myself walking along a cobble-stoned road which I recognised as Camp Hill in Birmingham. Then I found myself in the midst of a massive group of people walking towards Birmingham City's football ground, which was close by. Everything looked so different! The women wore long coats, laced up boots, and bonnets. The men also wore large boots, tight Edwardian trousers made out of quite course cloth, waistcoats, single breasted jackets and sported watch chains and flat hats, while some wore bowler hats. They could not see me as we crowded together, so it seemed that I had gone back in time. Whether Birmingham's football ground was built at that time, or whether the crowd was going to a fairground, probably where the football ground was later built, I had no idea. Next second I was back in my body in bed at home. *Fact or fiction?* Did I travel through time and space or was it a figment of my imagination? Another very interesting experience occurred many years ago when I found myself walking along a cliff top near the sea. It was a bright sunny day with the sun glinting on the waves and about five hundred feet below was a fine sandy beach. I remember running along the grass then sprinting towards the edge of the cliff, then leaping out into space like a skydiver. The air was rushing past me and I felt a sensation of falling from a great height. Then as I hurtled towards the ground, the only thing that flashed into my mind was whether I was in my physical or astral body because if I was in physical form, I had only a couple of seconds left to live. Then suddenly I was dancing across the beach, looking back up at the cliff top. I felt the fine sand beneath my feet and I was very relieved that I was actually astral travelling. Was that experience also imagination, a strong dream, or was I really flying and why was I able to analyse whether I was in physical or astral form, as I was hurtling towards the ground?

Both the USA and the Russians have conducted experiments in mind control which they call remote viewing. A suitable subject is selected then asked to concentrate on sending his or her consciousness to a specific location, observe a conversation between two people, and then return with the correct information. The object of course is to find out whether it is possible to obtain military information, which could be of value in a conflict. It could also help to save lives and win wars. I have no evidence that this experiment was successful. However, if it was, you can be sure that it would have been kept secret and placed into the realm of the official secrets act so that the press and public were left in ignorance. Who knows to what extent this kind of information, and the freedom it represents, is suppressed?

Can we really travel through time and space?
When I first became interested in astral travel, I often walked passed the Masonic temple near Kingsway, London, wondering what was inside. Then one night I attempted to channel my consciousness inside the building to see what was there. When I managed to get near the outer walls I found a force field preventing me from entering, but I could still see the floor covered with black and white squares before I shot back into my body. If the Multi Dimensional Universe does exist, then there must be many laws that the human race does not understand. Just go back two hundred years and ask yourself the same question, then check how many discoveries have been made that we were told would be 'impossible'. Now project your mind two hundred years into the future and tell me what will then be 'impossible'.

Chapter Seven
Transference of Consciousness

One day, in my capacity as an astrologer, advertising in Old Moore's Almanac and Prediction magazine, I received a call from a woman living in Chelsea who asked me to do a reading in her own home. The day before the consultation, I woke up in the middle of the night and there by the side of my bed was a woman's face, about four times the size of a human head. She had short blonde hair and large green eyes. There was no body just a head floating in space. Then she disappeared. Was I dreaming, or did a gateway open up from within the Multi Dimensional Universe? Was it hallucination or wishful thinking, and why just a head and not a body?

The next day I went to Chelsea and rang my client's bell, and when the door opened I had quite a shock because there in front of me was the very same person that visited me the night before. She was a stunningly beautiful woman who was very famous in her own right. She possessed great occult powers, which was quite apparent to me. I gave her a reading and left for Highgate, never expecting to see her again since she was in the process of moving overseas. Months later I cycled from Highgate to Lightwater in Surrey, to visit relatives, and after spending a very interesting evening, they asked me to stay the night and ride back home the following morning. Due to the fact that their two daughters had left home, they had a very large house all to themselves, so I was placed in one of the daughter's rooms.

After retiring, I stretched out on my back and went to sleep. There was a window on my right side. The curtains were drawn back so that some light filtered through into the bedroom. Then in the middle of the night, I was awakened, and became aware of a figure standing by the side of my bed. It was a woman silhouetted against the faint window light. I could not see her face, only an outline of her figure which I perceived out of the corner of my eyes. I was in a totally relaxed state, halfway between the dimensions of sleep and physical awareness which I had experienced many times before, when playing cricket, football and cycle racing. (Also, when I gazed over a gateway in Widdicombe, Devon, which I will describe later). I was in what could only be described as a catatonic trance. I was hardly breathing, but my brain was working overtime in an effort to perceive and understand what exactly was happening. Whenever an unusual paranormal experience occurs, I always attempt to find out whether I am awake or asleep, and in this case, I was wide awake but unable to move a muscle except the fingers of my left hand. I could not turn my head towards the window, but managed to peer out of the corner of my eyes. The woman was wearing a slip, which came halfway down her thighs, and then on looking upwards, I perceived that one strap of the slip had slid off her right shoulder, and I could also see that she had short hair that hung down and curved slightly under her chin. I knew that it was not the lady of the house, or either of her two daughters, so my visitor was either a burglar in physical form, a spirit entity that had passed on and returned, or I was in the presence of a physical materialization from the "Multi Dimensional Universe." Then I slipped back into a deep sleep, and the next thing I remembered was returning to partial consciousness, still in the original trance state.

I then found her lying face down, diagonally across the bed on top of me, with her feet stretched out to my left and her head on the pillow to my right. I could feel the weight of her body, the heat of her flesh and the silky touch of her slip, but I could not move a single muscle in my body except my left hand, which was resting on her naked buttocks. I probed and squeezed, then I felt the material of her slip, as well as the curved flesh of her buttocks. There was no response because both of us seemed to be physically paralyzed except that I could only move the fingers of my left hand. I estimated that she weighed about eight or nine stones and she was around five feet seven or eight inches tall. I kept asking. "Was I awake or dreaming?" "Was it wishful thinking or imagination?" "Was this manifestation really happening?" Then I asked the question through the medium of thought. "Who are you and what do you want?" There was no reply either physical or spiritual. Then I slid away into a deep dreamless sleep and when I woke up next morning she was gone. I sat down for breakfast in a very puzzled state, trying to analyse the events that happened during the night. Who was that woman and what did she want? Was it hallucination, wishful thinking or did a gateway open up through the "Multi Dimensional Universe?" I decided not to inform my hosts because many people are terrified of the possibility that such an event can actually happen. If it really happened, what else could be possible that we humans cannot understand? On my cycle ride back to London, the dawn of realization occurred as I came to the conclusion that it was the same lady that I had recently visited in Chelsea, who had since moved to the Bahamas. Later, she wrote a letter, asking me to come and stay with her. It was a magnificent offer that I was forced to turn down because my marriage had recently broken up, and I was left with the responsibility of bringing up a six-year-old boy on my own. She must have transcended the limitations of the physical body, transferred her consciousness from the Bahamas and then materialized in my room that night.

When I told a few of my friends in the local pub about my experiences, I became the brunt of hilarity because the majority of people just cannot accept that there are more things in heaven and earth, just as Shakespeare wrote in Hamlet. Is it possible to transfer consciousness onto the astral, then materialise on the physical plane? If this were possible, it would prove beyond doubt that the "Multi Dimensional Universe" is not a figment of the imagination.

Scientists have for many years, even before the days of Newton and Einstein, been attempting to find a mathematical formula for the mysteries of life, and the intricacies of the Universe. My contribution is to write down all my personal experiences, plus details of information gathered from friends and relatives, which could be interpreted by some thinkers as proof that other dimensions tangibly exist. I believe these dimensions break in to our everyday lives, often unexpectedly, and can be genuinely experienced. We may dismiss them as 'strange events' but they are nevertheless real.

The Ghost Dog of Honiton

Many years ago I went on a tour of Devon and Cornwall during which time a number of strange events occurred. On travelling towards Dartmoor, my vehicle suddenly spluttered and the engine stopped. On examining the vehicle, I came to the conclusion that my petrol pump was faulty. However, I managed to make a temporary repair which eventually took us to a nearby garage. Fortunately they were able to change the petrol pump, and then we set out to cross the moor, just as it was getting dusk. On passing through Honiton I was driving past a thick thorny hedge situated on the left side of the road, when I saw a massive hound looking at me from the middle of the hedge. It was black with one patch of light hair around one of its eyes. There was no gap in the hedge, so how could the animal have appeared half way in and half way out except in my imagination? Or had it transcended the known laws of the universe? Later I read an account that a ghost dog had been seen in the area of Honiton on the edge of Dartmoor. Could I have witnessed this so-called ghost dog? We carried on driving and dusk settled into pitch darkness. Then, as we turned a corner, there on the curve of the bend, was a sign by the roadside which said "Badgers Mount". Standing directly underneath was a live Badger with one of its paws raised as though to point the way ahead. By now we were very tired so we found a spot on the moor, parked the vehicle and went to sleep for the night. In the middle of the night I woke up with a start to find that the temperature had dropped, which was no big deal in the middle of Dartmoor, but I also perceived a presence just outside the vehicle, as though someone was watching. Eventually we went back to sleep and woke up with a mist swirling across the dawn landscape.

The sun rose, and the mist disappeared, so we set off on our journey, which turned out to be one of the most amazing days that I have ever experienced.

A Personal Glimpse of The Multi Dimensional Universe

It was a brilliant warm summer day as we approached Widicombe, the sun was high in the heavens, and the sky was a very deep blue with white billowing clouds drifting slowly across the horizon and a slight breeze caressing the tree tops. We stopped the car and right before me was a typical English farm gateway. I leaned up against the top bar and gazed out on to a most beautiful valley. In the distance I could see a few sheep and a number of cows all grazing peacefully. Birds flew overhead and insects droned as they flew back and forth. Then in the distance I saw a vehicle on the other side of the valley slowly making its way up to the crest of a hill. An aeroplane appeared in the sky giving the insects some competition with its engine droning as it passed overhead. My thoughts at that moment were projected to the absolute beauty of the English Countryside so I asked who designed this magical place? There was a blueprint for the plane droning overhead, a blueprint for the distant vehicle, a design for the farmhouse in the distance plus every item contained within its walls. There was also a blueprint for the very gate that I was leaning against, which had been designed by the creative talents of mankind. But where was the blueprint for the animals, birds, insects, and the human inhabitants of the valley?

Astral Vision

Suddenly the landscape reversed from positive to negative, just like looking at a photographic negative, yet the perspective remained exactly the same. Next moment I could actually see inside a nearby tree and beneath the green grassed turf and I was amazed at how much life it contained. Every inch of space appeared to contain a life form, then a great energy permeated my physical body, and for a few seconds I was shown eternity. Then I knew how the universe was designed, slotting together with such great precision. Everything was vibrating in a cosmic dance of life and death, all intermingling together. There was no such thing as space as we know it because all things were joined together, and the whole universe pulsated and vibrated with a massive cosmic love. Then slowly the negative vision changed back to positive, and for the next few minutes I stood in a trance, trying to remember what I had seen.

As I turned around my mind went blank and I could remember nothing except that I had been so privileged to witness "The Multi Dimensional Universe" in its full glory. I was never the same after that insight and all fear of life or death left me for good.

Chapter Eight
Does Prayer Work?

A recent TV programme was dedicated to finding out whether prayer works. An experiment was carried out in the USA using seven hundred-and-fifty patients suffering from heart ailments. People were separated into groups, some of which were prayed for by various organisations from different groups and religions. To start with no information was passed on to the patients, so they had no idea whether they were receiving the benefit of prayer. After a basic analysis of the results, there was very little difference between those patients prayed for and those without the benefit of prayer.

The next step was to separate another batch of patients, informing one section that they were the recipients of prayer groups working on their behalf, while the other section were given no information regarding what was going on. Again the results were inconclusive. But the one interesting point was how resistant a number of patients were against any form of prayer directed towards them from any source except their own religion.

Some psychologists involved in the study totally denounced the benefit of prayer, claiming that there is no proven scientific evidence. To be blunt, at the end of the experiment the doctors and scientists could find no correlation between patients that were cured or died due to prayer. I have seen TV programmes on the metaphysical world produced mainly by sceptics who always set out to disprove rather than look for the truth. For instance, a very good stage magician can create many illusions to fool the public. However, within the context of illusions, who is to say that an occasional real metaphysical event will not occur? Again on TV, a recent programme showed a stage magician performing various illusions such as levitation, moving objects without any form of physical contact, spirit communication with balls of light moving around in a darkened room, apparently without any human contact, and then finally dowsing with two moving sticks, all of which was explained by simple psychology.

Many years ago a couple of girls fooled the world with cut-out pictures of fairies which they placed in a garden, then rephotographed the images claiming that they were real fairies. It was years later they admitted that they had fooled the experts in the Victorian era.

To say that fairies do not exist because of a simple cut-out photography montage, which was proved to be false, is falling into the same trap as the sceptics. When so-called scientists denounce something as 'unproven', it usually means that they have not seriously examined the evidence from every conceivable angle. How can you prove that fairies do not exist? How can you prove that all dowsing is psychological? How can you prove that levitation is impossible? How can you prove that astrology is a figment of the imagination?

Having personally studied astrology for over forty years, I have never found one sceptic that has ever taken the trouble to learn the basic principles, and then study the events in a dozen peoples' lives to ascertain whether there is a correlation between the planets, and their individual behaviour on earth. Without a scientific study over a period of time, anyone who jumps to conclusions and has the audacity to call themselves scientists should be ashamed. Never in the history of the human race has any person written a paper or book after studying the basic principles of astrology, and then found that it did not work! The sceptical answer is that no person has ever proved its validity either, yet those same people always talk from a position of utter ignorance without any knowledge regarding the principles of astrology.

Years ago, I read an article in Fate magazine about an experiment that was carried out in France, not long after the Second World War. Scientists approached a group of criminals, who had been sentenced to death for murder, asking if they would consent to act as subjects for a medical experiment. They agreed to cooperate, and were sent to a hospital, then placed in beds where patients had died of cholera. The sheets and linen were not changed in any way since those patients had died. The criminals were given no information regarding this situation, and they did not develop any symptoms of cholera. Later they were removed from the ward and thoroughly examined for any contamination. All three were pronounced perfectly fit and free from infection. Then another three were placed in a sterile environment, with every precaution taken to ensure that no disease could penetrate their ward which was totally isolated from the rest of the hospital. They were informed that they were now in beds that were infected with cholera, and the last inhabitants had died from the disease. Even though there was no chance of them being infected, they all developed typical cholera symptoms and eventually died thinking that they were suffering from an incurable disease. The implications of these experiments indicate that prayer in reverse can influence the health of any person, in the same way that so-called black magic operates. As you think so you become. For instance, is it possible to control the throw of a dice by mind control? I have only had one personal experience of this phenomenon that took place at a party, years ago. The host was a compulsive gambler, and in the early hours of the morning he suggested that we play dice. He rattled the dice in a cup and we arranged to stake a small amount of money on each throw. I threw the highest number, and he upped the stakes for the next throw. When it was my turn, I concentrated on throwing a double six, and up it came. Then the game became very intense, as we continued to throw the dice over and over again, and I rolled the highest number nine times. I won every single throw until he gave up in sheer frustration. What are the odds of winning nine times in a row? I have never achieved such a large score before or since that evening; so what factors were operating which enabled me to run up such a vast score?

When I returned home, I looked up the planets positions to see whether there was any correlation between the behaviour pattern of the dice, my concentration, and what was happening in relation to my birth chart during that period. Yes, there was a correlation because the transiting Moon was conjunct my natal Saturn, which was situated at birth on the cusp of my eighth and ninth houses, in the sign of Capricorn, which was also a corner of what is called a grand trine that links the Sun and Moon together with Saturn.

Any planet crossing this point activates my subconscious mind, enabling me to influence the roll of a dice. This aspect could also have been in action when I concentrated on curing my appendicitis many years previously. Unfortunately, I did not keep a record of the date. What we term 'prayer' could at times be a form of self-hypnosis which triggers the subconscious mind into believing that a miracle will occur. On the other hand, if prayer is sincerely generated by a loving energy and service, its results may be miraculous. However, be very careful what you wish for intently because, under certain conditions, continuous visualisation, and verbal repetition of your wish could eventually manifest the object of your desire from the world of wishful thinking into the physical plane.

Jesus said: "Ask and it shall be given to you. Seek and you will find. Knock and the door will open." This is the very basic principle of how prayer works. All successful people use this system. First comes the idea, and then the inspiration to follow their desired path. Then they seek the knowledge to accomplish their goal in life. This is followed by visualization of the end product. When this is held in your subconscious mind you are asking the "Multi Dimensional Universe" to deliver the goods. Then when you seek success with action, doors will open for you.

"May the Blessing of The Cosmic Creator Be With You."

Chapter Nine
My Guardian Angel

When I was in my teens, almost every person rode a bicycle, and I was no exception. I joined the Solihull Cycling club and started to build what could only be described today, as a Tour de France racing bike. To finance the machine I sold my stamp collection, cut hedges, and looked for any local odd job that I could find, until eventually I had enough money for the project. Then I had a frame specially built, and all the parts were individually purchased and finally bolted together. I was so excited to set out on my first training ride with a friend called Alan Healey. As we rode down the main Birmingham, Warwick road, a Midland Red coach shot past as we were nearing Solihull, so we decided to sprint into the slip stream and coast along in its wake. We were hurtling along at about forty miles per hour when I attempted to change up to a higher gear without much success, obviously the gears needed adjustment so I glanced down to see why it did not change.

Suddenly I found myself lying in the middle of the road in a tangled mass of metal. As I slowly regained consciousness, I perceived a red post box and the coach, which had stopped fifty yards down the road. The driver got out, walked around to the back of his bus, looked it over then got back in and drove off, leaving me half unconscious sitting in the middle of the road. I started to move my fingers and hands then my feet and legs. I breathed in deeply, rolled my head left and right, and then slowly stood up looking for the blood. My beautiful new bike was a wreck. The front wheel was totally buckled, and the frame was twisted and bent. Then came the dawn of realization! I had struck the back of the bus at around forty miles per hour when it suddenly braked, so I must have shot over the handlebars, crashing head first into the rear of the bus.

Why I was still alive was amazing, but the most astonishing thing was that I did not have a single scratch, cut or bruise anywhere on my body, yet my lightweight racing bike was wrecked.

A force-field must have surrounded me that day preventing me from either being killed or seriously injured. Who or what was responsible for my miraculous escape? I could easily have broken my neck when my head struck the back of the bus. All I knew was that strange events often happened to me at regular intervals, and have continued all my life.

Later I realized that I had a guardian angel, and a spirit guide, to help me through the jungle of human life. I have seen the face and heard the voices, so I have no doubt that the "Multi Dimensional Universe" is a reality. After the strange events playing cricket and football, and the devastating cycle crash, another interesting event happened on a cycle training run between Birmingham and Coventry. I was training with about eight cyclists who were all using multiple gears, and I was the only one with a fixed wheel. When we crossed the main Birmingham Coventry road, I was leading the group, and then slowed up when approaching a halt sign. I stopped to check whether it was safe to proceed. The group changed down to lower gears and accelerated at a furious rate across the main road then climbed at speed up a long slope with a bridge at the top. Because I was riding a fairly large 77-inch fixed wheel, I could not get the bike rolling as fast as the group, so they left me standing. I toiled furiously in an attempt to catch up, but they were flying. I pulled up and leant on the bridge gasping for breath. The group were going hell for leather in the distance, doing what racing cyclists call bit and bit, with one person on the front of the bunch sprinting furiously for a couple of minutes then sliding off the front and dropping into the slip stream of the last person in the group. This meant that one rider on his own had no chance of catching a ferociously peddling group determined to burn the last rider off the end. I staggered off my bike and watched them getting smaller and smaller in the distance. "Oh well," I thought, "I have no chance of catching them tonight."

Suddenly a voice in my head said, "You are only beaten in life when you admit that you are beaten." The voice repeated itself, saying, "You are only beaten when you admit to failure. You can accomplish anything if you believe." So I strapped my feet back into the toe clips and, yelling like a banshee, I went berserk and hammered away like a steam engine. After about fifteen minutes, I looked up and saw that they were getting closer, and then slowly I clawed my way back to the last man in the bunch. A few minutes later I found myself leading the bunch, then one by one they started to drop like stones, until only two of us were left to finish the training run. The voice was right after all, and I have always believed that this principle of ultimate belief in life can overcome all obstacles. When I was seventeen, I was training for the first British under-eighteen Junior Massed Start Championship race, which was to be held at Gaydon airfield near Coventry. The Russell twins, Tony Denham and I comprised the racing team. One week before the event we decided on a very hard training schedule that included a course from Birmingham, Halesowen, Cleobury Mortimer, then over the Clee Hills and on to Ludlow. We rode like fury up every hill until we came to the one in four climb at the bottom of Clee Hill.

The other three riders all changed down to a very low gear, but I changed up to a 77-inch gear. This was absolutely stupid on a one-in-four steep climb. A strange event then happened. I felt light as a feather, as though the force of gravity had changed, so I stood up out of the saddle, and whilst the other three were gasping for breath, and without any exertion, I rode away from the other three leaving them standing in my wake. Five minutes later, when the mountain road flattened out to about one-in-seven or eight, Derek Russell and Tony Denham caught me up, and then Derek made a break with Tony and I trailing up the mountain together.

We reached Ludlow in that order, turned around and started our dash back at full speed. As we hurtled down the mountain, the sky was darkening, and a slight drizzle of rain occurred. I think we were travelling at least sixty or even seventy miles per hour, when I touched a wheel in front, then crashed on to my left side, with my feet still strapped on to the pedals. With my head skimming the tarmac, the force of the crash ripped off my jersey, until I eventually skidded to a halt. The boys stopped in the distance, rode back to help, and on regaining my feet, I continued on to Cleobury Mortimer, where a chemist patched me up, then we rode back to Birmingham.

It started raining heavily, and as we were negotiating an island, I skidded and fell off again. Eventually I managed to get home and went to bed. When I woke up next morning I found my left shoulder was terribly scarred. What stopped me from being seriously injured I never knew because we were travelling at more than sixty miles per hour down that mountain, so I believe it must have been my guardian angel or spirit guide looking after me. The race was held the following Saturday, but on Friday I developed a raging temperature and a dose of influenza, which kept me in bed for a week. I was lying in bed coughing furiously, when the sports news was broadcast over the radio. Derek Russell won the race and the title of Britain's first Junior Massed Start Champion. As far as I can remember, Tony Denham came fifth. What trick of fate stopped me riding in that race which I had so looked forward to for the previous six months?

My Spirit Guide

The first sight of my spirit guide occurred when my son Robert was around twelve years old. We were invited to the wedding of Peter Scott, a folk singer friend living in Swanage, Dorset. We booked into the Lulworth Cove Hotel, and then drove to Swanage for the wedding. At the reception, Peter's mother said that she thought he was doing the wrong thing by getting married. After the reception, Robert and I drove back to Lulworth and retired to our hotel. Then I decided to make a pot of tea and filled up the kettle. I plugged the lead into a wall switch then placed it right up against a large mirror, so when the kettle started to boil a jet of steam rose up and clouded the mirror. Suddenly a head wearing a turban, with a jewel in the centre, started to materialize in the mirror. My son was looking the other way, so very quietly I asked him to turn around and look at the mirror. His eyes stood out like organ stops. "It's a face," he gasped, as a tear ran down the face as though in sorrow possibly confirming the opinion of Peter's mother regarding his marriage.

On returning to London a month later, I received a phone call informing me that the marriage had lasted only three weeks, so the face in the mirror accurately depicted the forthcoming break. Could that face have belonged to my guardian angel or spirit guide, or was it a figment of my imagination? There were times during the 1960's when I used to attend a spiritualist meeting at the Foresters Hall in Kentish Town, where a medium named Joe Benjamin held court. During my first visit, Joe picked me out stating my surname. He then informed me that there was a man in spirit by the name of William sending his regards. How could he know my name, let alone the name of my grandfather who is long-since deceased? I confirmed the family name, also the name of my grandfather, and great grandfather.

On another occasion I arrived late, the hall was packed with not one empty seat in sight. As I stood looking around, Joe shouted to me: "Do come forward and sit on the stage." There were about eight people sitting facing the audience, and next to me was a young man who looked absolutely downcast, with an extremely low energy field. Then Joe started to go into his routine selecting people from the audience, giving messages and information about loved ones that had passed over, often giving exact names and locations. As I looked at the man sitting next to me, I decided to send him some love, light, and healing energy. I visualised a stream of light emanating from my aura, curving over to him so that he was surrounded by light and energy. There was no outward appearance because I was sitting quite still with my eyes partly shut as I concentrated on helping this man.

Suddenly Joe reached down and touched the man on his shoulder and said, "There is a person manifesting on the platform, recently passed over, who is a relation of yours, and she wants you to pull yourself together. There is also another person coming through, who says that she is your grandmother, and wants to thank the young man sitting next to you for sending power and light for her to come through from the other side." I nearly fell off the platform with shock because no person in that hall could have known what I was thinking at that time. Imagination or hallucination was not on since my thoughts had definitely been picked up by the medium, enabling another person to manifest on that platform. On numerous occasions, I booked a private reading with Joe Benjamin but I found him limited at individual sittings. To deliver precise information it seems that he needed the backing of massive group energy projected from the audience during his on-stage readings.

My Astrology Readings in Belgrave Square

Later, I booked a private reading at the Spiritualist Association in Belgrave Square, London, and saw a medium called Sylvia Crystal. She informed me that I should be doing readings at the Association, and suggested that I contacted the secretary offering my services. On arriving for my appointment, I bumped into Sylvia in the foyer, who pointed the way up the stairs to the secretary's office. I climbed up and knocked on the door. This was opened by a woman with a startled look on her face. The secretary was seated in front of a desk, and as he turned towards me I felt an odd, malevolent force emanating from both people. They looked at me as though I was the devil himself. "Go down stairs and wait in the foyer," the woman gasped, then slammed the door in my face. I had great difficulty in believing that such a ferocious energy had manifested from within that office. After about ten minutes, the secretary shot down the stairs and rushed out of the door into the street without saying a word, leaving me standing on my own. A few minutes later he returned and shot up the stairs. Eventually I was asked to make my way back to the office again. After a short interview I was booked in for a session of group readings using astrology as a basis for my work. When my series was completed, I decided that the vibrations of the organisation were not right for me, so I have never been back since that last day.

During a recent holiday to Cornwall, a friend who knew about my interest in the paranormal stated that he did not believe in ghosts or other dimensions. Then I explained that this physical life is really the world of illusion, and every person on the planet will at some time in their lives have had at least one or two glimpses of the "Multi Dimensional Universe". I said that, due to fear and the implications of what it could mean, many close up their creative thinking and avoid the whole subject. Then he told me a very interesting story that happened when on a cruise ship holiday with his family. A strange woman approached him and asked him where he came from. He said that he was from Cornwall, so she asked what area, and he replied, "Porth near Newquay." She then said. "Do you know Porth Veor Manor?" He replied, "I live almost next door." Then she said, "Do you know a woman called X who lives in Porth because I met her on a visit many years ago." The woman said that they had exchanged addresses but she lost the information. He was amazed because the woman named X was his mother-in-law. He gave the strange woman her address, made a note of her name and the cabin that she occupied. The next day he attempted to make contact again. After checking the passenger list and cabin number, he found that both did not exist on that ship. So the woman was undoubtedly a psychic manifestation from the "Multi Dimensional Universe."

Chapter Ten
My Fathers Return from the Dead

During Christmas 1967, my mother and father stayed in London for the festive season, and just before they returned to their home in Birmingham, my father and I went for a long walk on Hampstead Heath. As we were walking up Parliament Hill, he complained of feeling dizzy, and that this feeling had been quite persistent during the past few months. As long as I could remember my father suffered with migraines that always came upon him suddenly without warning, so that he had to lie down for a couple of hours. I know the feeling well, since when I was a child I suffered with bilious attacks. These left me shaking, sweating and unable to stand up. I was also subject to severe vomiting. Fortunately, when I reached my teen years the symptoms ended, but my father was never properly cured. After their return to Birmingham, I received a phone call from my mother at the end of January, stating that my father had been taken to hospital with severe head pains. This was eventually diagnosed as a brain tumour.

On his sixty-sixth birthday on February 16th, my father had a brain operation to remove the tumour. A few days later I went to see him at the Queen Elizabeth Hospital in Birmingham. He was sitting up in bed with his head bandaged. I asked him how he felt, and he replied that he was feeling better. I noticed that he was talking in a fast clipped Welsh accent, and was reaching out with his hands, as though attempting to touch or stroke someone. I asked what he was doing, and he said that he was trying to touch the dog. "What dog?" I asked. "The dog at the bottom of the bed," he replied, continuing to reach out as though stroking an invisible hound. He then mentioned the name of Nell, which was his sister-in-law's name. On talking to his brother Frank, I mentioned my father's behaviour and wondered why he used the name Nell, also the black dog at the bottom of the bed. "Oh," said Frank, "When your father was twenty-one, he had a black dog called Nell, which was probably what he was seeing at the bottom of the bed." Was that an illusion, or had his pet dog returned from the grave to greet him, and help him over the barrier between the physical and spiritual world? At the end of February 1968, I received a call from my mother saying that my father had deteriorated, and could I come up to Birmingham right away. Immediately I drove up and saw my father, who appeared very weak and was suffering with breathing problems. I really did not know what to say, so I asked him what he had for breakfast, and as always he came up with a joke. He replied, "Pick my teeth and see what's there." On the 6th of March 1968 at lunchtime, I went once again to the hospital, and my father had been placed in a bed at the very end of the ward; which tells its own story. He was very drowsy, so I touched him and he opened his eyes. When he looked at me, I saw a totally different person to the father that I had known all my life. His eyes glowed and sparkled like diamonds, and his mouth turned up in a slight smile. He seemed to gaze directly into my soul with the most loving and knowing look that I have ever witnessed in a human being. It was just as though I was looking into the face of an Archangel. He was in reality reading my future with an all seeing eye, which sent a shiver up my spine. "Do you know what is happening," I said. "Yes," he replied. "I am dying." I did not know what to say, so I muttered. "Are you afraid?" "Oh No," he replied, and then closed his eyes. My mother and I were just about to leave when she turned to me and said, "He wants to kiss you goodbye." I turned and saw him looking at me, puckering his lips for that final last kiss. I held his head and kissed him for the last time. Then he sighed and went back to sleep. The next visiting time was about six thirty in the evening, so my mother and I brought a close friend along to visit my father. At around 6.20 pm we were nearing the hospital, when my right foot became very heavy, as though there was a weight pressing down on the accelerator. The car seemed to have a life of its own as it sped along at a furious rate, well above the speed limit. Then when we drove into the car park at the Queen Elizabeth Hospital, it was a very calm still night with not a breath of air circulating around the tops of the trees. We parked the car, proceeded into the hospital and found a lift which took us to the top floor. On getting out of the lift, a nursing sister approached and said, "Please ask you mother and friend to go into the waiting room, and will you please come with me." She ushered me into a room where my father lay on his deathbed.

"I am sorry," she said, "Your father passed away at 6.30 pm." This was just about the time that I felt a pressure on my foot increasing the speed of the car, as though he was saying. "Get a move on, I am on my way." I leaned forward and kissed him on his forehead, then walked back along the corridor towards the waiting room to inform my mother that he had gone. Then a most amazing event happened - one minute it was dead calm outside then suddenly the hospital was battered by a violent wind-storm which roared around the building, rattling the windows, and buffeting trees and walls. It felt like a tornado was circling the building, then as suddenly as it started, the wind dropped leaving the hospital completely dead calm. There are many instances recorded in history that when a person of power leaves this world a great storm often occurs. For instance in September 1658 when Oliver Cromwell died, there was a massive storm raging over Britain, uprooting trees and causing considerable damage. When the Red Indian chief Crazy Horse died, the sky went black, and a great storm appeared. I knew that this was my father's way of telling me that he was at last free of the physical world. This was confirmed later that same night, when I was awakened with my father shouting my name so loud that I nearly leapt six feet into the air with shock. He had returned to tell me that there was no death, and that he was still alive in another dimension.

So the "Multi Dimensional Universe" did exist after all.
Once again the unbelievers will pronounce their version of these events, however, as I have always stated to many sceptics:
"You will have the shock of your life, when one day you wake up and find yourself dead."

When my son was born, he had many characteristics of both grandfathers, and when he was around three or four years of age, one night he climbed out of his cot and marched into the lounge with his special blanket over his shoulder. "What is it Robert?" I said. "Man in my room," he said, "Taps me on the wrist and wakes me up." I took him back to bed and asked for a description of the said man. "Wears glasses, a flat hat and a raincoat." This was exactly what my father wore when we went to watch Aston Villa play football. I informed Robert that it was his grandfather coming to see him from the other dimension, and when he felt a tap on his wrist that it was grandfather telling him that he was being looked after, and that no harm would ever come his way. "Oh," the boy said, "that is all right." He then went back to sleep with great confidence. His father looked after him during the day, and his grandfather protected him at night.

Before my father died, I made a record of his palm prints, since having studied palmistry for many years, and out of curiosity, I wanted to see whether a brain tumour could be diagnosed from a hand print. Sure enough, on one hand was a complete break in his line of mentality. A great island formation on the other palm also suggested that all was not well in the area ruled by the brain. In other words it was possible to diagnose brain damage by the lines on his hand. There will be more information on palmistry later in a special chapter.

Another Return from the Dead

Another instance of a return from beyond the grave occurred when a local woman in her mid seventies died and returned after death. For many years I helped this woman after her husband died by looking after her car when she went on holiday, then driving her to the coach station and back again. She had no children of her own, and often complained of back pains which was eventually diagnosed as cancer of the spine. When she was in hospital I went to visit her, and she asked me to find out how much her old car was worth because she did not think she would ever drive it again. I made numerous enquiries and checked the guidebooks for the best price.

I was informed that the car could be worth anywhere from fifty to five or six hundred pounds, with a maximum value of around seven hundred and fifty pounds depending on its condition. The mechanics were in a reasonable condition, but the vehicle really needed a respray. I conveyed this information to the said lady, informing her that my son was looking for a second hand car, so I offered her the top price of £750 without any argument. Her reply was absolutely amazing since here was a woman dying of cancer, with a considerable amount of money in stocks and shares. She replied, "If I can't get a better offer, you can have the car for £750."

What on earth was she thinking? I had helped this woman on many occasions, and she did not trust me one inch to give her an honest assessment regarding the value of her car. I laughed and left the hospital, but when I went to see her a couple of days later, she had obviously asked another friend to assess its value because she said, "You can have the car for £750." So I gave her a cheque to conclude the deal. Then she asked me whether she could get a refund on the insurance policy and the tax disc. I felt desperately sorry for that poor soul and offered to enquire. The insurance and tax disc was valid only for the next four weeks, so I contacted the insurance company who laughed out loud at my request. When I conveyed this information to her, she then asked for a refund for the petrol in the tank. I informed her that I had put the last twenty pounds worth of petrol in the tank, and never asked her for the money.

A few days later she died, and was buried with her husband. The next night, I awakened from a deep sleep, finding myself in that half-and-half state of complete relaxation which usually occurs when any paranormal experience happens. Then the woman flew through the wall behind my bed, wearing a white shroud with earth dropping from it. As she floated up near the ceiling, I found myself out of the body, right up against the ceiling in the opposite corner. I knew that she was trying to take me with her, so I pushed power and said, "No I am not coming with you." Then she disappeared, so I slipped back into my body, and went back to sleep.

Another Amazing Encounter

Recently I experienced an amazing encounter in a small cottage in Ramsgate, Kent. I was meditating by myself, sitting upright in an armchair. As my vibrations slowed up, I went into a semi trance with my physical body in a state of extreme relaxation. Then I heard a sound like a gust of wind arriving from the top right hand corner of the room. Suddenly a figure appeared sitting in a chair, slightly in front and to my left. I perceived a very large man with massive wide shoulders, wearing a light brown cloak. His face was pointing away from me, and on his head was a very strange hat, with the sides and back turned up, and a long point at the front about eight inches long. It was the type of hat worn in the middle ages by a person of importance. There were no adverse vibrations so I assumed that he had arrived to give me the once over as a suitable person to be sitting in that particular space and house. Then he disappeared. Many years ago, the house was probably situated within the original precincts of the local Abbey. Perhaps I was privileged to receive a visit from the Abbott or high official who once lived in the area, or had a special responsibility for it.

Chapter Eleven
Information from Police Files

Many years ago a friend was working on night duty as a desk sergeant in London's West End central police station, when a frantic woman screamed down the phone. "Officer, Officer, my walls are moving." "Yes madam," the sergeant said, "I will send an officer around immediately." He then detailed an available constable to visit the hysterical lady, whose flat was situated very close the police station. The constable was invited in and questioned the lady regarding which walls were moving. "That wall," she replied, pointing to a wall situated next to her bed. The officer noted that there was no activity, and the walls were still and solid, so he returned to the police station and filed his report. An hour later the woman was back on the phone even more hysterical, so the sergeant sent another constable to visit the woman, and he too returned with the same report, which was also filed. Then every half an hour the woman telephoned with even more hysteria. "My walls and windows are moving, please do something officer!" she screamed. Then two very experienced detectives entered the station, so the sergeant asked them to do him a favour, and sort out the hysterical woman once and for all. They knocked on her door and were invited in to her flat. They examined the walls and bay windows which were quite solid and immovable. Then one officer asked the woman exactly where she was standing when the walls moved. "I was in bed," she replied. "Ok," the detective said. "Would you mind getting into bed so that we can see whether anything happens whilst you are lying down?" As she slipped between the sheets, the detectives reeled back with shock. The hair stood up on the back of their necks, as the temperature in the room suddenly dropped. Then the walls started moving as though they were made out of a flexible material, not solid brick. The bay window also moved like water flowing over a shallow river. One officer placed his hands on the wall and the bay windows, but they still moved under his touching hands. "Bloody hell!" gasped the officer as he staggered back and sat down in a large armchair at the other end of the room. The moment he sat down, it rose up off the floor, and with the officer still seated, it flew across the room a couple of feet off the ground and landed by the widow which was still moving in a dance with the vibrating wall. The officer leapt out of the chair like a scalded cat, then screamed at the woman to get out of bed. The minute her feet touched the ground, the walls and windows stopped moving. "Grab hold of the bed," he yelled to the other officer, and then they lifted it across the room and placed it in another position. "Madam," the officer cried, "please get into bed." When she climbed back between the sheets, the walls and windows stopped moving. "Problem solved," the detective gasped, then they both dashed out of the door, and on returning to the police station, filed their report, after which there was no further telephone calls from the frantic woman in question.

A Police Task Force

Another very interesting piece of information came from a talk with my friendly desk sergeant. After he was promoted to the rank of inspector, a special task force was set up giving him authority to travel anywhere in London, with a selection of highly experienced officers, in an un-marked transit van. He would often stand on the pavement near traffic lights observing passing motorists, then radio to his team a few hundred yards along the road to stop a particular vehicle.

Time after time, he found that his team were making such a stir in the force with a vast number of criminals arrested for all kinds of offences: possession of illegal drugs, stolen property, carrying guns, drinking and driving, no licence or insurance. At the end of every patrol, they were the most successful team in the British Police force. One evening, four of his officers asked him whether they could spend the night in a derelict building in the East End of London, so he off-loaded them for the night. They found a table and some chairs inside the building, lit candles and played cards for a couple of hours. Then they heard a vehicle pull up outside, so they doused the candles and waited in silence. Sure enough, a couple of men entered the building with suitcases full of stolen property, and when they opened up the cases, the officers switched on their torches and arrested the thieves.

Suddenly this group of highly successful task force officers was disbanded, and no explanation was given. The answer must have come from the top echelons in government, not the police force. So why disband such a successful task force? Obviously, they were catching too many ethnic criminals, with one particular group most active. The lunatic, liberal, woolly-minded do-gooders could not stand reading the statistics. They pushed their crazy, politically correct, racist rubbish, to get the group disbanded. Recently I read that due to government pressure, an unmarked vehicle was using stealth tactics by the police to catch speeding motorists. When honest citizens are targeted instead of criminals, it will eventually be the start of the revolution. Already a group of honest citizens declared war on the police, by destroying over seven hundred speed cameras. In France irate farmers and angry motorists often blitz speed cameras. Sooner or later this may also happen on a much larger scale in Britain.

The present Labour Government has targeted motorists with speeding fines, parking fines, bus lane fines, congestion charges, and possibly future motorway tolls. The police and government have introduced a system of indirect taxes to prop up the financial failures of national and local governments. At the same time we are informed that thousands of criminals are driving without tax or insurance. They are allowed by the present law to burgle and mug victims, in their own houses, and law-abiding citizens cannot properly defend themselves, in case the poor criminal gets injured.

One lunatic politician recently appeared on TV stating that householders should not take the law into their own hands because he did not like the idea of young teenage burglars being severely injured, if the householder defends himself and his family. And to prove how out of touch this woolly-minded unearthed politician was, he stated that it came under the same principle that if a motorist knocked a child down the parents would then have the right to take the law into their own hands. How can any intelligent person compare the legality of a burglar, with malice aforethought, breaking into a house in the middle of the night, and possibly mugging, raping, torturing, or killing their prospective victims for personal gain with that of the motorist? So if the burglar is injured in the process do they have the right to sue the householder? To classify both events under the same banner proves beyond doubt that the lunatics are no longer in the asylum, they are now in the British Government. Either the law has to be changed, or eventually there will be some sort of revolution. **"Those whom the Gods destroy they first make mad,"** and we in Britain are plagued by the human rights act, which unpractical, woolly-minded, liberal do-gooders, and the criminal element, have exploited to absolute maximum effect. Now they are targeting honest British citizens who want to celebrate Christmas, and have asked for a Christian Cross to be removed from a register office because it might cause offence to ethnic minorities. A report in the national press recently exposed a nursery school that changed a long-standing children's nursery rhyme from "Ba, Ba, Black Sheep" to "Ba, Ba, Rainbow Sheep" because it was a politically incorrect statement for "Equal Opportunities," and gave the wrong impression to children at a very early age. For God sake, can we not have some common sense, instead of the vicious bullying tactics to destroy the British way of life?

If you check the statistics, you will find that we in Britain are not so much a multi-racial society, like the woolly-minded unearthed politicians would like to ram down our throats, because the total ethnic community, covering all races and religions, makes up less than ten percent of the population. Also when it comes to breaking the law, certain ethnic groups top the list by a massive percentage for criminal activities per head of the population. It is also sadly true that only one section of British society is responsible for the terrible crime of suicide bombing.

The police and government know about these facts but the authorities seem petrified to stand up and be counted. By not pinpointing the perpetrators because of political correctness, racism, and using the term "equal opportunities," we are playing with fire in the long term. Also by opening our borders to all and sundry, the government is responsible for so much criminal behaviour perpetrated by illegal overseas asylum seekers. We are so weak on crime that many vicious criminals are given light sentences then let out of prison to commit further crimes. This is due to the human rights law brought in by the Brussels bureaucrats which protects the rights of criminals, but not that of law abiding citizens. How much more betrayal can we in Britain take from this New Fascist Labour Government?

Chapter Twelve
Unidentified Flying Objects

The bible contains references of an unidentified flying object which was referred to as a flying roll; so what we call flying saucers have probably been seen for thousands of years. In fact, there are so many reported sightings of unusual flying objects that even if ninety-nine percent are hoaxes, the other one percent could well be factual. For instance, there were many recorded sightings of UFOs years before the first plane had left the ground. On January 1st 1254, a UFO was seen by monks at St. Albans in Hertfordshire, England, and was described as a large flying ship. In 1290, the monks at Byland Abbey, Yorkshire, England, witnessed a large silver disc flying over the Abbey. On August 7th 1566, massive glowing discs were seen over Basle, Switzerland. On December 11th 1741, Lord Beauchamp witnessed a ball of fire hovering over London before zooming upwards with smoke trailing behind, as it disappeared into the sky. On September 7th 1820, a vast number of objects were seen flying in formation over the French town of Embrun. More than 10,000 people reported that they had seen a large airship hovering over Kansas City, Missouri, USA in 1897. On 21st April 1897, Alexander Hamilton, a member of the House of Representatives, made a sworn statement, that he was awakened by a strange noise outside his house in Le Roy, Kansas, USA, and witnessed a cigar shaped flying object about 300 feet long, brilliantly lit and occupied by six very strange figures; it landed and later shot off up into the night sky. There have been not hundreds but thousands of sightings around the world during the last milenium, with the majority of sightings recorded at the end of the 19th and early 20th Century, and right up to the present day.

For instance, a friend once worked as an air hostess after the Second World War. As the plane was flying into New York airport, she looked out of the window of the small passenger plane, and only a short distance away was a round shimmering disc, keeping pace with the plane. All the passengers saw it. Suddenly, it dipped out of sight underneath the plane, and shot up on the other side. She dashed into the pilot's cabin informing him what she had seen, but the captain simply said, "Take no notice, they follow us all the time. We do not report these incidents because no one believes us, and the authorities would ground us on the assumption that we were having hallucinations." So no report was filed. I personally have witnessed a silver disc hovering in the sky when I was travelling from London to Reading by train. As I looked out of the window, the disc was about the size of my little finger nail so I assumed that it was some sort of balloon. Then the train hurtled into a cutting, and when it came out the other side, the disc had disappeared within about five seconds. The sky was cloudless and clear blue, so where did that disc go in such a short space of time.

In the 1970's, I was involved with the Arts Theatre Club. The manager, Tom, one night had an argument with his girl friend, then climbed up on to the roof of the building overlooking Great Newport Street, in the West End of London. As it was a warm night in summer, he opened a deck chair and stretched out. After dozing off to sleep, he suddenly woke up and saw a formation of silver discs, shaped like an arrow, hurtling across the London sky. They were travelling so fast that they went from horizon to horizon within a few seconds. According to Tom they must have been travelling at well over five thousand miles per hour. After a short space of time they re-appeared at an angle of ninety degrees, and once again flew across the London sky before disappearing into the night. Were they in physical or astral form, and did they come from outer or inner space? Was this event imagination, hallucination, or a manifestation of the "Multi Dimensional Universe"?

Around about that same time in the mid 1970's, I was informed by two local boys living in Highgate, North London, that one dark night they saw a great silver disc hovering over Langbourne Avenue. They both dashed indoors to tell their parents, who rushed out in order to see for themselves, but by then the disc had disappeared. Obviously the adults totally disbelieved their children. Years later, one of the lads told me exactly how it happened, and he appeared extremely sincere in his belief of what he and his friends had witnessed.

Some UFO sightings have been verified by eye witnesses on the ground, whilst at the same time being tracked on radar, and then seen by pilots sent to intercept, before the UFO shot off up into the sky at a speed that no modern war plane could match. Another friend, June was staying the weekend in a very isolated house near the south coast. In the middle of the night, the house started to vibrate and her bedroom was illuminated with a very bright light. She jumped out of bed and saw that a pulsating giant disc was hovering very close to the roof, illuminating the whole house. After a short period it moved away then shot up into the sky and disappeared. The friend that she was staying with also saw the UFO.

The great question is not whether they exist because the evidence is overwhelming, but where do they come from? Are they spacecraft developed on earth by the human race? Or have they come from some remote underground or underwater city built by extra terrestrials? Perhaps they could even be a different genetic race that has survived on earth for thousands of years? Could they even be vehicles that can travel through time and space and live in the "Multi Dimensional Universe" with the ability to materialize and de-materialize at will? Your guess is as good as mine.

The British Ministry of Defence

However, the British Ministry of Defence started a UFO project between 1991 and 1994 code-named Project Condign. Today, under the freedom of information act, The Ministry of Defence have published a former secret report on UFOs. It is the most highly classified report on the subject ever released, and originally only eleven copies were made. The report states that, in 1950, the chief scientific advisor in the MOD, Sir Henry Tizard said that sightings should not be dismissed without a proper scientific study. Originally the people involved in research thought that UFOs were just hoaxes or delusions. The report also says that, in 1952, when Winston Churchill was Prime Minister, he asked for information about UFOs and was informed that they 'were no threat to security'. Later that same year there were a number of UFO encounters which were tracked on radar. Fighters were sent to intercept, and pilots reported visual sightings before the UFOs sped through the sky and shot off at a speed that modern aircraft could not match. The military, private pilots and the police reported sightings of the craft. Between 1976 and 1978 there were over one thousand sightings recorded. On December 26th 1980, a UFO reportedly landed in Rendlesham Forest, very close to two USA air bases at Bentwaters and Woodbridge. One military witness touched the hull of the ship and sketched some of the Egyptian looking symbols. Indentations were later found on the ground corresponding to the location of the UFO. Geiger counter readings were taken and radiation was found to be considerably higher than the surrounding countryside. The UFO returned the following night and was witnessed by the USA Deputy Base Commander, Lieutenant Colonel Charles Hait.

On March 30th 1990, a UFO was seen over Belgium, and two F-16 fighters were sent to intercept. After locking on to the craft with their on-board radar, the UFO danced about the sky playing cat and mouse with the fighters before shooting off into the sky at breakneck speed. On November 5th 1990, two RAF Tornado planes were flying over the North Sea when a UFO suddenly appeared alongside one of the aircrafts, before it accelerated away like a rocket. On March 30th 1993, a vast number of sightings occurred over the UK, including a massive triangular craft seen flying over RAF bases at Cosford and Shawbury. Witnesses saw a UFO hundreds of feet in diameter emitting a low frequency sound as it moved slowly over the countryside, before shooting off into space many times faster that any known aircraft. On January 6th 1995, a UFO came dangerously close to a Boeing 737 on its approach to Manchester airport.

As Shakespeare wrote in Hamlet, "There are more things in heaven and earth Horatio, than are dreamt of in your philosophy." Could this be an echo of: "In my Father's house there are many mansions"? Who is to say what is fact and what is fiction? Once upon a time we were told that the earth was flat, and that if we travelled far enough we would fall off the edge.

Recently a Channel Five programme was broadcast on UFOs in the most amateur way that could be imagined, with ridiculous whispering, hushed voiceover and strange, supposedly 'spooky' music. This turned the programme into a farce, with the voiceover barely audible. It was advertised as a serious TV documentary, and some idiot director ruined the show by introducing this fantasy voice and weird music, which seriously detracted from credible reporting.

Another Genuine Reported Sighting
In another reported incident, three flying discs approached a small plane. The pilots reported the sighting while still flying, and the discs were tracked on radar. When the plane landed, the authorities separated the two pilots, keeping them apart for many hours. They were then informed that they were not to speak about what they had seen. This system of hiding the facts from the public has been going on for many years. I believe that the only reason some incidents are being reported, and documents released, is because the world's governments have decided to prepare the public for possible future contact with aliens from the stars to avoid panic. There are billions of stars in the universe, with probably millions of planets supporting some type of intelligent life in all areas of development, from very primitive life forms to super-intelligent advanced beings.

I maintain that the Earth has definitely been under observation for millions of years, otherwise there would have been no UFO sightings. Where they come from and what they want has not yet been established. At present we are much too primitive and violent for any advanced alien race to make open contact because, after watching the human race slaughtering and persecuting one another for the past few thousand years, any advanced race would keep their distance, and observe our behaviour from afar, probably with total amazement.

Darwin discovered the theory of evolution, stating that living creatures evolved over millions of years in order to survive on this planet. Because one theory is accepted as fact, it does not mean that another totally different theory is wrong. Could they both be right? Certain life forms that we call human could have developed from apes, and on the other hand, we could just be a great experiment conducted by Gods or scientists from another universe or dimension. Perhaps they played games to see who could invent and produce a specific DNA that would eventually develop into the dominating race on planet earth? If all the millions of life forms on this planet were designed and sent here from another dimension, where does that place the world's religions? Does God really exist, or is God just the excuse that violent men use to control the masses? There is no doubt that a power source and intelligence exists throughout the universe. Exactly what and where is its source of energy and power?

Chapter Thirteen
Death of a Football Team

Every year, the same group of teams in the premiership challenge for the British championship. The media becomes saturated with information; games will be analysed and debated in great detail. Will it be Manchester United, Arsenal, Chelsea or Liverpool, this or any other season? Can these four teams continue their great success, or will one of the outsiders make the running next season? As a football fan, I will be glued to the TV with anticipation, yet at the same time I will be sad, because every Sunday morning for over twenty six years, starting in the early 1970's, Dartmouth Park United played soccer on Hampstead Heath, London, come rain, mud, snow or hailstorms. Today the old pitch is overgrown, and has now been turned back into a meadow. Twenty-five years ago, dozens of games were played on Hampstead Heath every Sunday morning. Now it is almost deserted, as though amateur football has become a forgotten game.

Regardless of playing conditions, we turned out to kick a football, even when the pitches were too waterlogged to play. Then we scoured the Heath for firm ground, and set up training bags for goalposts. We played in snow blizzards, with drifts two feet deep, so that we could hardly lift one foot in front of the other. Many times during the last few years, I stood alone on our old pitch, tuning in to past sounds of ferocious tackles, crashing bodies, and shrieking players swearing at each other, as though it was a war we were fighting, not a football game. Perhaps in a hundred years, a local person walking a dog late at night, may hear the ghostly sounds of our late football team, playing a celestial game for all eternity, through time and space.

Dick Turpin once held up coaches passing through Hampstead Heath, and often stayed at the Spaniards Inn, Hampstead Lane. The Romans, probably defeated Boudica, somewhere between Hampstead Heath and Kings Cross, though no one knows exactly where that last battle took place. The once famous Dartmouth Park United FC, is now as dead as Dick Turpin and Boudica, though we may all have shared the same area of ground. Local magistrate and lecturer John Carrier, author Hunter

Davies, and a variety of local celebrities founded the club in order to kick the week's stress out of their systems. There was no referee, no offside rules, and decisions were made by the group as a whole. At times we had thirteen a side, and even ran a smaller five-a-side game nearby for latecomers. During the 1970's and 1980's, there were always at least a dozen games in progress on Hampstead Heath every Sunday morning. Now it is deserted! Could this be because it costs over three hundred pounds or more per season to hire the pitch, or has football lost its appeal?

When we started, the team list looked like a page from who's who, with TV's Melvin Bragg, now Lord Bragg, film director Gerry Harrison and Bernard Donougue, now Lord Donougue, who was financial adviser to Harold Wilson when he was Prime Minister. On one occasion Gerry Harrison was in the House of Lords, on a visit in connection with his film work, when Bernard appeared strutting down a corridor. "What are you doing here," said Gerry. "I'm supposed to be here," said Bernard, "I'm a bloody Lord." A policeman standing nearby almost had a fit at the repartee between the two Sunday footballers. The team continuously changed over the years, as numerous members retired for all kinds of reasons, and new blood appeared, and I mean real blood because if you think it was a bunch of aged amateurs who stood about posing, you would be very much mistaken.

The game was taken so seriously that we had violent arguments with punches thrown, and players carried off with broken legs, damaged knees, concussed heads, and some of the tackles would have made Vinny Jones run for cover. Steve Mcfadden, who plays Phil in East Enders, was also a member of the club.

My first game occurred in 1978 after playing indoor five-a-side soccer for seventeen years. I started my first game on a waterlogged pitch covered with soft mud. I was selected for the treatment, which consisted of being body checked by one player, then having my legs simultaneously swept from underneath me. After the tenth battering, I received the ball and flew past both antagonists, and then I heard a most ferocious snorting and stamping right behind me, as though a huge bull was pounding in my wake. Once again my legs were scythed from under me, and the human bull leapt over my mud-covered body. For the first time in my life, I reacted with malice and charged towards my tormentor with fists raised to do battle. As we squared up on the mud soaked pitch, two players grabbed my arms, and two restrained them, making it much too difficult to deliver blows, until we calmed down sufficiently to simply snarl and growl at each other. One Sunday morning, we arrived at our pitch to find the Russian Trade Delegation playing the Russian Embassy on our hallowed ground. I dashed on to the pitch and shouted, "Bugger Off, this is our pitch." The referee turned around and said, "Yes, what do you want, I am Boogerough."

At half time during one game, Hunter Davies announced that he was opening a bottle of Champagn because I had reached the ripe old age of fifty and was still playing football. He produced a set of glasses and dished out the bubbly. We had a couple of Russians playing their first game who at first refused to accept a glass, thinking that the decadent British always drank Champagn at half time. Then we explained that it was tradition to open a bottle of bubbly for anyone still playing on reaching fifty years of age.

One of our teams often played a back four, with a combined age of nearly two hundred and forty years. However, we were not all old coffin dodgers because many youngsters played from early teens, twenties, thirties, forties, and many retired early finding the pace too fast and the game too rough. We sported players that had trials for many professional clubs, and one member played professional football in Portugal. At times we were like the League of Nations with members from the USA, Brazil, Argentina, Canada, France, Germany, Holland, and Belgium, Italy, Sweden, Denmark, Russia and numerous African countries. They were mainly students taking courses in Britain or working here on a contract. We had Lawyers, Window Cleaners, Accountants, Musicians, Carpenters, Taxi Drivers, Actors, Politicians, Lecturers, Film Directors, Photographers, Publishers, Stock Brokers, Wine Waiters, Brick Layers, Tree Surgeons, Doctors, Writers and Motor Mechanics. You name a trade or profession, and they have at some time or other played for Dartmouth Park United FC.

We had one player nicknamed Metal Mickey, who in his forties could out-play and out-run any of the youngsters. However, he was quite eccentric, wanting to fight everyone on the pitch. On one occasion I was playing in goal when the ball came my way. I attempted to kick it clear and it landed in front of the opposition's striker. He grinned like a Cheshire cat and banged it past me into the net for a goal. Metal Mickey who was playing on my side went berserk because my clearance fell short. Up went his fists as he dashed towards me mouthing obscenities. "I will finish you off," he screamed. "Mickey," I shouted, "I am on your side, the opposition is over there, go and flatten them." After a considerable exchange of insults and further threats of violence, I walked off the pitch, leaving Mickey foaming at the mouth. This ferocious behaviour continued for many months, so one day after a game I asked him what was his problem. "Why are you so aggressive every Sunday?" I said, and he replied, "You don't have to live with my wife." So now we knew why? On another occasion a very well known person, a pillar of the local community, went berserk and swung a vicious left hook at one of the opposition, fortunately he ducked just in time otherwise the force of the blow would have taken his head off.

One Sunday morning we were about to set up the posts when a stranger with a large dog appeared. One of our players had brought his small five-year-old daughter to watch the game, when suddenly the dog pounced knocking her to the ground. We pulled it off and yelled for the owner to control his animal, which he refused to do. It then leapt at the child for a second time, who by now was terrified, screaming her head off. Then Ted, our top striker came dashing up proving that he could strike with his fists as well as his feet. He walloped the offending dog owner with a right hook that Mike Tyson would have been proud of. His glasses flew in one direction and he in another, eventually he staggered to his feet, placed his dog on a lead and threatened legal action for assault, but later thought better of it and dropped the charges. We had our own Lawyers, Solicitors and Magistrates for him to contend with, and we had asked him politely, to restrain his animal before our striker intervened.

On another occasion, we were short of players, when four people appeared on the horizon, two men and two girls. "We are visitors from Sweden," one said, "Any chance of a game?" "Ok!" we said. "Get changed." Our jaws dropped when the girls removed their trousers, and shouted for the ball. The two fellows looked puzzled at our reactions. "Have you never played with women before?" one said. "Not on a football pitch," I replied.

After twenty-five years the team split up because less and less players turned up each Sunday, so I wondered if the end of the world was imminent because I can't think of anything else that could have caused the demise of Dartmouth Park United FC.

The Elemental World

One dark night many years later, a very interesting event occurred by the side of the old football pitch. Sometimes I went for a walk around Hampstead Heath in the middle of the night, and on this occasion I stopped by the old oak tree under which most of the team changed into their football kit. I placed my hands on the tree and then started to breathe deeply and meditate.

An oak tree has great power, and will help to remove any emotional turmoil, replacing it with a constructive spiritual energy. The emblem of the ancient Druids is an oak tree for a very good reason. As I stood perfectly still, with both hands placed on the tree, I became aware of about a dozen pinpoints of light shimmering within the trunk of the tree. Automatically I assumed that they were reflections from something behind, above, or to the side of me. I turned around and saw nothing that could have reflected on to the tree. When I turned back they were still there, directly opposite my chest. For a few minutes they continued shimmering like stars on a clear night and then disappeared.

Chapter Fourteen
The Highgate Vampire

During the last thirty years, journalists and sensation seekers, attempting to attract publicity, have written about the Highgate Vampire. When I first came to live next door to the cemetery in 1960, it was totally neglected and overgrown with foliage and weeds. Tombs were left open, and one could walk in and browse around without interference. The catacombs are fantastic, and some of the mausoleums looked as though they were built for an Egyptian Pharaoh. At the very highest point in Highgate Cemetery, about one thousand feet above sea level, is the mausoleum of Julius Beer, a Victorian multi-millionaire, who paid the equivalent today of around three million pounds for his last resting place. There is always a succession of Chinese and Russian visitors looking for the tomb of Karl Marx, which is situated in the new east wing. However, the old burial grounds containing the catacombs are situated on the west side of Swains Lane, which runs from Highgate village through the centre of the cemetery, down to Parliament Hill Fields where it meets Highgate West Hill. The Cemetery was consecrated by the Bishop of London on 20th May 1839, and was part of seven modern burial grounds around the city because graveyards attached to most churches were overflowing with corpses, and were seen as a health hazard.

The first person buried in Highgate Cemetery on 26th May 1839 was 36-year-old Elizabeth Jackson, who died in Soho, London. The east side of the cemetery was opened in 1854, and it is here that Karl Marx resides with a massive marble bust indicating his last resting place. There are six Lord Mayors of London, 48 Fellows of The Royal Society, and hundreds of famous Victorians planted here. Edward Hodges Bailey, who sculpted Nelson in Trafalgar Square; Rowland Hill, who invented the postal services; Michael Faraday, who invented the electric generator, which formed the foundation of modern electromagnetic technology; William Friese-Greene, who invented moving pictures and then patented the system (but the production of the camera made him bankrupt so he sold the patent for £500 to cover his debts). When he died, on the hour of his funeral, all the cinema houses in Britain halted their films for two minutes' silence in respect for his great achievement. The world famous sculptor Henry Moore is also buried in Highgate Cemetery.

A Modern Day Vampire Hunt

During the early 1970's two so-called vampire hunters, Sean Manchester and David Farrant, pranced around the cemetery looking for the undead. The publicity generated resulted in the cemetery coming under siege one Halloween night from thousands of young would-be vampire hunters, sporting mallets and stakes. The police were helpless to restore order because the colossal volume of would-be vampire hunters left a trail of destruction behind. The next day the place looked like a battlefield. Sean Manchester claimed that he found a vampire in the cemetery, and then pursued it to a Gothic style house in Muswell Hill where he drove a stake through its heart, causing its body to disintegrate as it turned to dust. David Farrant was in the cemetery, when a group of youngsters started desecrating the tombs. The police were called and he was charged with the offence, even though he was not involved. He claimed that the police falsified the evidence to get him convicted. Eventually a friend purchased the cemetery for one pound, and turned it over to a committee who made it into a commercial success. Visitors now pay to enter, which means that money can be spent on upkeep, and security guards with dogs patrol the grounds to stop further desecration.

Do Vampires Really Exist?

Do Dracula-style vampires really exist, or are they created by imaginative novelists hoping to make a few pounds? We all know the true story regarding the witches of Salem in America, where a group of young girls threw themselves screaming and kicking on to the floor. This was instantly attributed to witchcraft. Once the girls were pressurized by the elders of the community to denounce the source of their possession, they realized the power they possessed, and they named any person that had previously offended them. So great was the hysteria generated, that innocent people were hanged! The blood-sucking vampire was made famous by three main authors. First, by John Polidori who published a book called "The Vampyre" in 1819, which in 1820 became a great success as a play in Paris. Second came "Varney the Vampyre" by James Malcolm Rymer, which was published in 1847, and was on the best sellers list for about fifteen years. Finally, in 1897, the most famous vampire of all was "Count Dracula" by Bram Stoker, who was originally a civil servant in Dublin, and a part-time drama critic. He then became the business manager for the great actor Henry Irving. Bram Stoker was seriously involved with show business before he researched and wrote Dracula. However, when it was scripted into a play, Henry Irving turned it down, and never played Dracula on the stage. Karl Marx referred to both vampires and were-wolves in his description of the ruling classes, describing the people as victims, though it was not blood he was discussing, it was slave labour.

To give you an idea how legends start, the following two stories can be interpreted in many different ways. One dark night I was walking down Swains Lane from Highgate Village, when I perceived a short grotesque bow legged figure scuttling along in front of me. As we approached the cemetery, the figure leapt into the air and vaulted over the fence into Waterlow Park, which lies adjacent to the new east cemetery, and then disappeared into the night. The lane was very dark with no streetlights, so I could only see an outline of the figure. When I recounted my tale in the local public house, of possibly meeting the Highgate Vampire, the crowd erupted with laughter because the grotesque figure belonged to a very eccentric woman, who did nude modelling at art colleges.

On another occasion whilst walking down the lane one very dark night, on top of the cemetery wall, well above my head, was a huge black figure which looked like a typical Hollywood Vampire. It appeared to be wearing a massive black cloak which was spread out either side of its head, like great bat wings. It was very dark so I could only see an outline of the creature. It then let out a most terrifying, ear piercing scream as it flapped its wings. I ran like hell, with its screams echoing down the lane, in the wake of my pounding feet. Next day I walked back up the lane in broad daylight, and on top of the massive cemetery wall, was a huge peacock, which was obviously the very same creature that made such a din the night before. One afternoon when I was passing the cemetery, I perceived a tall figure wearing a black full-length cloak, and a large dark wide brimmed hat, standing in front of an open tomb. Suddenly the figure turned and entered the tomb, so I shot through the gate, and followed it into the building. The figure turned, looked me up and down and said, "Hello, I'm in charge, and the owners of the crypt have allowed us to set up an office inside, to sell postcards and cemetery paraphernalia." We chatted for about half an hour, and then he asked me whether I had booked my plot in the cemetery. "Good Lord No," I replied, "I am not dead." "I have booked my plot," he said. "I have purchased a tombstone covered with moss, with my name inscribed." I replied. "Have you had the date of your burial chiselled on the stone?" "Not yet," he replied, "I am still alive, but I have taken out an insurance policy, which will enable me to be conveyed to my grave in a glass topped hearse, pulled by four black horses, with plumed head-dresses and a police escort.

Visitations from the Cemetery

Within a few months of moving into my flat overlooking the cemetery, it became like Piccadilly Circus in the rush hour, with entities from the other dimension, zooming in and out during the night. One night I stayed up late and then went to sleep on a bed settee in the lounge. In the middle of the night I was awakened by heavy footsteps pounding along the hall passageway. A number of intruders entered my lounge, paused by the side of my bed settee, which had two wooden arms either side of the bed, about a couple of feet high. My head was underneath the blanket so I could not see a thing. My natural instinct was to roll sideways out of the bed and leap to my feet, ready to do battle, but the wooden arms were in the way. I presumed that if I moved the intruders might be armed and dangerous. I could hear their deep heavy breathing and shuffling feet moving about by the side of my bed. I kept perfectly still, with every hair on my body standing up like barbed wire. Then, after about thirty seconds, they charged out of the lounge and thundered down the other passageway leading to the bathroom from where there is no exit. As they left the room, I leapt about six feet into the air, totally convinced that they were burglars in physical form that had somehow opened my front door without me hearing their entry. I snarled furiously, and dashed after them to do battle. My wife rushed out of the bedroom screaming, "What is all this noise?" "Where are they?" I gasped, peering behind every door, and looking in all the cupboards. "Where are who?" she yelled. "The mob that just ran through this flat," I howled. We searched the place from top to bottom, but there was no trace of a forced entry, so we came to the conclusion that the intruders came directly from the cemetery, then went back as fast as they had arrived after giving us the once-over. My concern then was to identify the intruders. Were they Vampires looking for a quick bite, or were they elementals on the prowl, or could they just be curious spirits giving us the once-over? My scientific friends scoffed, refusing to believe that I had experienced contact with another dimension. "You were dreaming," they said. "Your imagination ran riot." The interesting point here is that I have absolutely no fear of contact with the other side. My critical Virgo mentality, plus my training as a professional photographer, works on the basis of observation and analysis, so in almost all cases of contact, I am in a completely relaxed state, halfway between sleep and waking. This is when most psychic phenomena occur. Afterwards I sat down quietly to analyse the event, and make notes for future reference.

An Attack by a Real Vampire

If you think that was scary, what happened next was even worse. A few months later, my wife went to visit her family, so I was left on my own. I was fast asleep in bed lying on my back, and as I slowly started to awaken, I heard a strange twittering sound in the distance. I was in that dream-like state of complete relaxation, half way between consciousness and sleep, where every muscle feels warm and limp, and I could not move even the slightest fingertip. The twittering grew louder, exactly like the sound-track of a film called "Night of the Demon," where a great horned figure emerged from a cloud of smoke, growing larger and larger until it was as big as a train. The musical director was obviously familiar with the sound of an approaching entity because he reproduced it in the film with great precision.

Due to my previous studies in psychic self-defence, I knew exactly what to expect as it passed through the wall and landed on my legs, then rolled up over my body and started to smother me. I could not breathe or move one single finger and was fast losing consciousness! It felt as though I was being drowned. As a last resort I called on a higher power to assist me in my quest for breath because all I needed was one large breath of air, and then I could do the rest. Suddenly my lungs started working, so I sucked in a large draft of air which enabled me to focus my concentration, re-activating my physical body. I pushed power from my solar plexus chakra, which is ruled by the fire element, sat up in bed then projected a most ferocious burst of astral fire, directly at the elemental vampire. When you visualize a picture in your mind, it is instantly created on the astral plane, so with one more colossal mind projection, using the fire element, I singed its butt, propelling it violently back to the cemetery where it belonged.

The next night I sat up for many hours because I had a premonition that it would return. Lo and behold, about 3.30 am, I heard it twittering in the distance like a flock of birds. It came ever closer, slid through the wall, and entered my bedroom. Only this time I was ready. As it approached the bottom of my bed, I breathed deeply, pushed full power from my solar plexus chakra, and then sent a ferocious blast of astral fire in its direction. It let out a scream, and shot out of my flat, followed by the fireball that I had created by the concentrated power of mind force.

After that episode I erected a protective barrier, preventing any further intrusion into my flat during the hours of darkness. Just inside and above my front door; I pinned the tarot card, ace of swords, with the blade pointing upwards; a silver pentagram was placed over the top of my front door, and a corn dolly was attached to one side, plus a painting of an Egyptian Ankh, over the door into my lounge. I also placed a psychic portrait of the Archangel Uriel, ruling the magical world, including electronics, computers, aviation and maths, in my lounge over the door facing the front entrance. Also a copy was placed in my bedroom over the fireplace, and in my garage. Then I sprinkled each wall, door and window with holy water, sealing off my flat from any further astral interference. On the lower floor of my block of flats lived an elderly lady, who also was an avid reader of occult literature, and one evening she contacted me and said that she kept hearing a twittering and buzzing noise in her flat at night. It was a similar sound to what I had experienced upstairs, so I set up a protective barrier in her flat to prevent the elemental Vampire from crossing her threshold, and to the best of my knowledge it never returned.

Local Vampire Experiences
On making enquiries, I found out that many people living close to the cemetery had similar experiences, where they were attacked during

the night then found themselves drained of energy the next morning. A local lady said that she woke up one night, and found a small grotesque creature, something like a gargoyle sitting at the bottom of her bed. She screamed with fright, the creature disappeared and never came back. Another local woman stated that in broad daylight, a tall figure of a man wearing a long cloak appeared in her lounge, yet the door never opened. He then walked towards the wall and just disappeared right through it, as though it was not there. The same woman also stated that she had removed a shelf over her fireplace, enabling her to push a couch back against the wall. Early one morning she suddenly observed a woman in her flat arranging items on the very shelf that she had removed. The shelf was not there in the physical plane; but was visible on the astral including the ghostly figure of a strange woman. She also informed me that when she was working as a nurse, one night she went to sleep in the hospital, which was situated very close to Highgate Cemetery. She half woke up in the middle of the night finding a strange figure with its head on her neck. Then in the morning another nurse asked her what was wrong with her neck. On looking in the mirror, she found a number of very small incisions in the side of her neck.

Now, was Sean Manchester right or wrong to claim that a vampire existed in the cemetery? My own personal belief is that there have always been psychologically disturbed people who drank human blood, but it has never to my knowledge been proved that these depraved people lived hundreds of years by the infusion of new blood. However, it may be medically possible to remain looking younger because, a continued regular transfusion of young new blood could possibly retard the ageing process, enabling a so-called vampire to retain its youth, but for how long is another matter. I have heard of athletes having a blood transfusion before a special race, which may enable them to increase their oxygen intake, thereby improving performance. Vampires or elementals can exist in physical or astral form, and usually drain off your energy not blood. An elemental vampire can take over a human being by operating through the physical body of its victim without the host knowing what is going on. The physical vampire is usually a different form of life altogether but has the same effect of draining all your energy, leaving you very depleted. The important signs to recognize an elemental in human form is that it has no morality whatsoever, causing mayhem in every direction, and when it can't get its own way after using every trick in the book, it will develop a ferocious rage, and often become violent. It will never be on time for an appointment, tell every lie imaginable, and have no regard for any living person except itself. Throughout history, violent entities have gained positions of power in society, then proceeded to wreck havoc on the human race. They always fall in the end because the Law of Karma, which is the law of God, manifests through words and behaviour patterns, returning all words and deeds back where they came from. So by their own actions they eventually destroy themselves.

How to Identify a Physical Vampire

To help you identify a physical vampire or werewolf within your circle of family and friends, listen to the sound of their voices. If they continuously rabbit! rabbit! rabbit! in a soft monotonous voice, without a pause for hours on end, almost sending you to sleep, you are in the presence of a human vampire that will drain your energy, leaving you feeling limp and exhausted. Another syndrome for identification, are well meaning friends that will not take no for an answer. They persist in demanding your attention and presence, without any thought that you may be busy with other things. This type of vampire is often a very psychologically disturbed person, and has had severe emotional problems in their early years, and is now dumping their problems on you possibly without realizing that they are draining your energy banks by their constant attention.

Stalkers and obscene phone callers are a form of vampire because they have no regard for another person's privacy, and create fear and apprehension in their victims. The werewolf type makes a totally different approach, projecting a sudden ferocious verbal or physical attack that leaves you terrified and totally drained of energy. You can always identify this type of assault because it strikes you in the solar plexus, leaving you feeling sick and lifeless, sometimes shaking so much that you can hardly stand up. We have all experienced at some time in our lives such attacks, and felt the power of the vampire and werewolf syndrome. A personal relative had a great battle with her mother, who was living in the marital house. The husband studied martial arts, and often ran about at night in bare feet to toughen up the soles of his feet. The mother thought that this behaviour was terrible, and verbally battered him with such hatred that eventually she was instrumental in splitting up the husband and wife. I personally heard her say "I hate him", over and over again, long after he had left home. On one occasion when I visited the family, the wife who was over forty years of age said, "Ask the old dragon whether you can take me out to the local pub for a drink." The mother was quite happy for me to take her daughter around to the local pub. Then, as we left, the wife said that the only way she could see her husband was for somebody like me to take her out, so that she could meet him secretly without the mother knowing. He was banned from entering the family home by this ferocious werewolf mentality of his mother-in-law. The couple were eventually divorced and later, when the mother died, the husband moved back to the family home, and they re-married. Today they are still living happily together.

Now here is a very interesting event, which happened a few years later. The wife was in bed one night, when she was awakened by a presence and, on looking up, saw her mother at the bottom of the bed as solid as she was in life. The mother spoke quietly and said that she was so sorry for all the heartache that she has caused, and she hoped that they would be much happier from now on. Then she disappeared, never to return. Hallucination, imagination, wishful thinking, or was it a doorway into the "Multi Dimensional Universe" through which that person materialized from the astral into the physical dimension? Deep breathing and prayer will help to counteract the destructive forces let loose on the unsuspecting. A study of psychic self defence will also help to identify the assailant – which, sad to say, could be any member of your family or circle of friends.

A Different Type of Encounter

One dark night about two in the morning, I heard a bang outside my flat in Swains Lane. Since I rented a garage backing into the lane that had previously been burgled, costing me £400 worth of camping gear, I was hopping mad. I assumed that the burglars had come back to finish the job, and clear out my garage. I slipped on a black tracksuit and trainers, and then hurtled down the stairs to do battle. On peering out into the lane, I perceived a small open-topped sports car, coasting down by the side of the cemetery, with a pair of legs protruding out of the back. There were no lights or engine noise. Then as it approached Chester Road on the south side of the cemetery, three figures jumped out of the car and proceeded to push it around the corner. They travelled about fifty yards and were obviously attempting to get it started, so I climbed on to the cemetery wall which was about three feet high. By holding on to the spiked railings, towering about nine feet high, I was able to approach silently and unobserved.

When I was about six feet from the three villains, I screamed at the top of my voice and leapt as high in the air as I could. With one accord they turned their heads and looked up into the air. From the low angle of their viewpoint, it probably appeared that I had jumped right out of the cemetery, bounding over a nine-foot fence. I stood upright and growled, "I am the Highgate Vampire, and I haven't had my dinner." Never have I seen three more startled expressions on human faces, as they jumped from that car. Their heads twisted sideways, and their eyeballs stood out like organ stops, as they sprinted down the lane at a rate of knots that even Linford Christie at his best would have been hard pressed to match. I snarled and roared, then chased them along Chester Road until they disappeared into a narrow alleyway. I then retuned home and went to bed, knowing that it was not my garage that was under attack.

An affinity with the Animal Kingdom

Living next door to the cemetery has been an education, not just because of manifestations from the other dimension, but also because of the interesting events taking place within the animal kingdom. One dark night while walking up Swains Lane, there in front of me was a small owl sitting on a fence, about three feet from my face. It did not move, so I said "Hello Owl". It turned its head and stared with unblinking and immovable eyes then silently it flew back to the cemetery. On another occasion after departing from the local pub, I heard a scraping noise when a shadow flew over a six feet high fence, touched my head, and then bounded off down the road. It had a long bushy tail, a pointed snout, and was about the size of a small dog. As it hurtled down the road, it sounded like a small galloping horse. Then it leapt up over the cemetery railings and loped off into the night. Around midnight, I was walking near the cemetery, when a giant rat crawled slowly across Swains Lane, then slid between the railings in

Bromwich Avenue. When it was just inside, it stood up on its hind legs, turned towards me, rubbed its paws together, and made a chattering sound. It was a massive rodent, with a tail about two feet long. I stooped down about three feet from the creature and chatted back. Then we began a conversation in rat language, though I had no idea of what we were talking about. I said in English. "Hello Rat, how are you?" Then he turned sideways and crawled away into the night. One day when I entered my block of flats, I found a ginger cat lying on the stairs. It was almost dead and as thin as a rake. When I picked it up, it just looked at me with very sad eyes. It was a large full-grown animal with a very thick coat, but it was vastly undernourished. I took it into my flat and laid it down on a cushion, then placed a saucer of milk nearby, but it was too exhausted to move. When I woke up the next morning it was still alive, though it had not moved. I phoned the local vet, who called in and examined the said moggie, then pronounced that it was probably too far-gone to save. However, he said that he could fill it full of penicillin, and hope for the best. He came back many times, and the cat seemed to improve, and it started to drink some milk. That cat never left my flat for six weeks, whilst I fed it and attempted to heal the beast until eventually it returned to fitness, put on weight and padded around the flat. It was obviously a wild cat, so one evening I carried it down the fire escape and set it free in the back garden. After stalking and sniffing through the trees and bushes, it slid through the railings and headed for the cemetery. It crossed the road and climbed into the graveyard. Then I witnessed one of the most amazing spectacles that I have ever seen in my life. The sun was very bright and low in the sky, throwing an outline of fire around the cat as it sniffed the air. The cat stood up on its hind legs and rubbed its neck against the branches of a nearby bush. As it turned towards me, it had a smile on its face like the proverbial Cheshire cat, and then it danced away, still on its hind legs, with a look of ecstasy on its face. The sunlight illuminated its dancing figure before it disappeared into the dark recesses of the cemetery. I staggered back with great sadness because I never expected to see my friend ever again. However, later that night I walked into the lane and whistled a few times, then as I was about to give up I heard a meow in the distance, Moggyvitch as we called him, jumped out of the cemetery and followed me up the fire escape back into his new home. Then we had a cat flap cut in the back door, so that he could come and go as he pleased. He could roam about the cemetery at will, and always came back home when I whistled, probably to get his supper. He lived with us for a few more years. Then one afternoon when I was walking up through the Holly Lodge Estate there on the grass verge was my beautiful ginger Moggie, lying on his side with his legs outstretched, like a racehorse jumping over a fence. I touched his body, and he was dead and stiff as a board. He had obviously been run over by a car, and was instantly killed. I carried him home, and with great sadness he was buried in the back garden that he loved so much. We once had a cat called Bingo, who used to jump on my stomach when I was sleeping on the couch. If I dropped off for a nap, I would wake up with a start when he jumped off the back of the sofa and leapt on to my belly, using it as a springboard. I was quite used to Bingo's weight landing on me numerous times during a week. He was with us for many year, but then one day he never returned, so I presumed that he had an accident and was dead. A few years later, when I was dozing on my couch, I woke with a start, as I felt the weight of Bingo landing on and jumping off my stomach. I sat up and looked around, but he was nowhere to be seen. There was no doubt in my mind that he was still with us in astral form, and had visited to let me know that he was still alive somewhere in "The Multi Dimensional Universe."

Over the years I have given shelter to five different cats that loved the freedom of living in the vicinity of Highgate Cemetery. After the last cat had departed, I still left the cat flap in place just in case another moggie took a shine to my flat. And that is exactly what happened, though not the way that I had visualized. A giant cat called Cassius occupied the floor below. For some strange reason, Cassius took a great dislike to me, and was the only animal that ever attempted to attack me. One night when I was fast asleep in bed I woke with a start and heard a creak, then in the low level illumination I looked up and witnessed my wardrobe door opening. My first reaction was that a burglar had entered the flat and was in the process of helping himself to my property. I leapt out of bed with a growl, then I heard the patter of bounding feet in the passageway, followed by a click as the cat flap opened and shut as the burglar shot out onto the fire escape, then back in to its own home downstairs. Every night the same thing happened, so I balanced plates on the edge of the kitchen table, then if it jumped up it would knock the plates off, and frighten itself into leaving me alone. Alas the strategy did not work, and for night after night I was plagued with the strolling moggie stomping around my flat. Eventually I hit on a very cunning plan, which was to tie up the cat flap with thick string so that it could enter from the outside, but would not be able to get out afterwards. Then I could possibly persuade the said moggie to vacate my flat permanently. The next night it entered as usual, marched around the flat then when I eventually got up to give it a piece of my mind, I had the shock of my life because the cat had undone the knots that I had tied using its teeth, then departed as usual. I had great difficulty believing that this cat could reason how to open the cat flap by untying the string with its teeth. It did not bite through the string, it just untied half a dozen knots to make its escape.

Within a short time the owner left Highgate, and took the said moggie with her, so the problem was solved. When a person's spiritual consciousness develops, the animal kingdom seems to understand that a rapport exists. For instance we have a squirrel living nearby which we call Nutkin. This creature often sees me from across the road, and when I whistle and hold up a nut, it sits up on its hind legs, holds its paws together, and then scuttles towards me. When I sit down on the grass nearby, it creeps closer and closer, then climbs up on to my leg, takes the nut out of my hand and sits on my thigh eating the nut. Then for its next trick, it climbs up my arm and sits on my shoulder whilst eating the second nut before scampering away and zooming up the nearest tall tree. I often placed a few nuts in the branches of a local tree, and a few hours later they have always disappeared. I often wondered where squirrels lived, and on one occasion I saw a creature with its mouth full of leaves. Suddenly it shot up to the top of a tree and disappeared into a nest.

At times I have found many injured creatures on Hampstead Heath, including a black rabbit, which had obviously been abandoned after the Christmas period. It had no chance of survival if left to its own devices because it was obviously a tame creature. So I caught it and took it to the animal sanctuary in nearby Waterlow Park. Again I found a crow with a damaged wing attempting to hide from predatory dogs, so I managed to catch it and deliver it to the Park for safe keeping. One amazing experience occurred one morning when I was driving up Swains Lane. Just by the cemetery gates there is a massive twelve to fifteen foot wall on the left side, and a much lower wooden fence leading to Waterlow Park on the right. Suddenly, a duck stood up on top of the wall, and flew across the road into the park. Then a vast number of minute yellow ducklings leapt off the wall into the roadway. I stopped the car and blocked the road, with irate motorists honking away, but I took no notice and, on leaping out of my vehicle, I gathered up at least a dozen ducklings and popped them into my car, then drove off. Later I took them into the park and reunited them with the mother duck that was swimming on the local pond. We often have a family of foxes sleeping in our back garden in bright sunlight, which is overgrown with bushes and foliage, so they cannot be seen from ground level. However, being on the top floor, I can see them clearly basking in the sunlight. At night they bark and yelp as they pass through the garden on their way back to the cemetery where they obviously have their den.

Early one morning a friend looked out of my window and could not believe her eyes. Loping through the foliage was a very large brown cat about the size of a Great Dane, with a small head, small pointed ears and a long tail. It loped away and obviously disappeared back into the cemetery where it lived. To date no other person has seen this large cat, so it must keep a very low profile and only comes out at night. One afternoon I was sitting in my lounge, with the two top windows wide open when a small blue bird, the size of a sparrow, flew into my lounge and crashed against the opposite wall. It then dropped flat on its back with its legs in the air. I thought it was dead, but when I picked it up, held it in my hand, and breathed on it, the creature stirred and moved its wings. After about ten minutes it came back to life, so I placed it outside my bathroom window on a gutter ledge, then it flew away. The next day I opened the windows and sat down overlooking the garden when suddenly, to my astonishment, the same blue bird flew into my flat through one window, as if to say thank you for helping me. It then flew straight out of the other window, never to be seen again. Once I was walking past the cemetery when I heard a great squawking in the trees, and on looking up, witnessed a large crow with a sparrow in its beak, zooming in and out of the branches, pursued by half a dozen sparrows, obviously attempting to peck the crow in order to get it to release its victim. No matter where the crow flew, it was pursued and pecked at by the furious collection of smaller birds until it let go of its prey. Only then did the cacophony cease, with the birds singing together, chirping out their victory song.

Many years ago, on a very dark night, I was travelling along a narrow road in the depth of the countryside. In the headlights of my car, I saw a small young bounding bunny. As I approached it ran through a cutting with grassy banks about nine feet either side. Then it turned sideways and attempted to climb up the slope. I stopped the car, and as it tried to reach the top it fell back, so I grabbed it and lifted it up the bank and popped it over the fence into a safe green field. When I picked it up it squealed, assuming that I was looking for my dinner, but I assured it that I was well-fed and had no claims on its person. Then it hopped away into the night. A similar event happened when I was travelling late at night through a Hertfordshire country village. As I left the houses behind, and continued along a dark country lane, a giant brown hare with huge ears and massive legs shot into the lane just in front of my car, then proceeded to bound along in my headlights for about sixty seconds. Suddenly it turned right and leapt right over a six-foot hedge into a darkened field and disappeared into the night. If you send out vibrations of love and affection you will always receive visitations from the animal kingdom regardless of whether they are dangerous or harmless.

A Close Encounter

One Indian friend born in Kashmir said that when she was a little girl her parents told her if she was ever accosted by a wild animal not to look it in the eyes, but to stand perfectly still until the danger departed. To scream or run could be fatal. Then one day she and her small brother were walking alone through the jungle when a great Bengal Tiger suddenly appeared right in front of them. She held her brother's hand very tightly, and stood perfectly still. The great beast ambled up and sniffed them both at close range. She said that its head towered way above them, and its sudden intake of breath a few inches from their faces sounded like a roaring wind. Then as suddenly as it appeared, it turned away and loped off into the jungle, leaving them both dumbstruck with fright.

Chapter Fifteen
Psychological Analysis using Palmistry, Astrology, Tarot

Palmistry, Astrology and the Tarot are all examples of ancient teachings which so many western people denounce as fiction. However, with one accord, I have not ever come across any person denouncing these ancient arts who knew the first thing about the subjects they so ferociously denounce. How many universities include these ancient subjects in their curriculum when teaching psychology? To my knowledge the answer is virtually none! Jung, Klein, Winnicott and Freud are covered by most courses, but the introduction of either Astrology or Palmistry in order to arrive at a carefully prepared psychological analysis is looked on as some sort of abomination. Many academics appear to be blind, with tunnel vision, to anything outside the normal system of teaching. Fear and religion is usually the problem. However, to my knowledge, there is only one psychology teaching course in Britain that starts lessons by lighting a candle and saying prayers for protection. They also include details of the seven chakras, and teach the value of how different colours affect a person's health.

When dealing with any disturbed person, their thoughts can be very destructive, and a psychotherapist needs personal protection, which can be obtained by lighting a candle, meditation and prayer.

At a party I was introduced to a well-spoken man who was once a photographer. He had returned to university, and eventually became a doctor. When the hostess stated that I was studying astrology, this person jumped back a couple of feet then scurried to the other side of the room as though I was the devil himself. After making enquiries, I found out that he was well and truly tied up with a religion that forbade the study of astrology, yet as a doctor he could have used these ancient arts in combination with conventional medicine in order to obtain a more accurate assessment of any patient. The truth of course will set you free, but that is not what conventional political correctness, or fundamental religion is all about. On another occasion I was having a drink with a business friend when the subject of astrology came up, which he vehemently denounced as fiction. When my friend was well and truly inebriated, I asked him why he did not believe. His answer was very interesting because he said that he would hate to think that any person could predict his future behaviour pattern. So in reality he was afraid of the truth, regardless of his personal belief. Every child in school knows the name of Sir Isaac Newton who spent fifteen years exploring the possibility of finding the philosopher's stone, by changing lead into gold, apparently without success. However, he eventually discovered the system of calculus and the law of gravity. On one occasion, he was accosted by a scientist at the Royal Society, who derided Newton for studying and reading astrology charts, stating the subject was a work of fiction and totally unproven. Newton, who had spent many years studying the theory of astrology answered with the following statement. "Sir, I have studied the subject and you have not." There is no answer to any argument, if the person denouncing a subject is talking from a position of ignorance, and it seems to me that, in many instances, the more educated a person becomes, the more the ego expands and, for some unknown reason, their thinking becomes extremely fixed.

Another scientist who used astrology was Kepler, who actually invented what is called the minor aspects because he was not aware of the three outer planets at that time in history. Yet the amazing thing is that when I was at school all traces of their experiments and writings regarding astrology, and the metaphysical world, were removed from the history books. What else has been removed? Right through history, books and scrolls containing occult knowledge have been destroyed or banned by religious and political bigots, in order to keep the public under control, by instilling their own brand of fear. It is so easy to pronounce material to be 'rubbish' if you have been brainwashed by a conventional religion or philosophy into disbelieving that which you cannot understand. The Jesuit tradition says: "Give us a child in its first seven years, and it will be ours forever." This is in reality an admission that a child can be brainwashed and controlled in order to increase the power of the group mind. This is achieved by pumping a specific philosophy into the child and society, regardless of whether it is fact or fiction. To counteract this devious and destructive philosophy, when my son Robert was a small child, I said to him. "Adults will very rarely give you helpful advice. Never take too much notice of what you are told, always politely listen to another point of view, then analyse why they are making that particular statement. If it is not advantageous for you to follow that path, take no notice and go your own way." Any group philosophy, whether it is religious, political, legal or commercial, will always pump home their particular version of the truth which may or may not be correct. When any organization is exposed to the truth, which it wants to deny, it will always close ranks and attempt to destroy the source of exposure. Therefore, you will never learn what is fact and what is fiction by attaching to any group, regardless of what they call themselves. The truth is out there, and you must find it on your own without any outside group brainwashing. When I was living in Birmingham, most people looked on me as deluded because of my basic beliefs, so I thought that maybe I was heading for the asylum. Eventually I left the midlands for London and, lo and behold, I started to meet numerous kindred souls with similar experiences.

My real education to understand the "Multi Dimensional Universe" started through reading Fate and Prediction Magazine. Every month there appeared numerous articles, which documented the very subjects that I found most interesting: Astrology, Palmistry, Psychology, Tarot, Magic, Religion, Flying Saucers, Dowsing, the I Ching, and many more unusual subjects. The authors I read were John Naylor, John Pendragon, Madeline Montalban, Alfred Douglas, Jo Sheriden, and many other occult writers. I recommend that any student of metaphysics research these authors. Suddenly I was not alone in thinking that there was more to life than the material world. That in itself was a bit of magic because I often thought that I was crazy to believe in a "Multi Dimensional Universe."

When I was a child and looked up into the night sky and saw the glittering heavens on a clear night, I always believed that we came originally from the stars. The scientists now tell us that the earth was formed by stardust, around four and a half billion years ago, and as it cooled down, the DNA code implanted in every living thing somehow evolved out of next to nothing and eventually produced millions of different species. How then could a human footprint wearing stitched sandals be found within the footprint of a massive dinosaur, laid down sixty five million years ago? If this is true then the history of the planet is vastly different from what we have been taught.

The Basic Principles of Palmistry

Palmistry was the first metaphysical subject that I studied seriously. I found that the shape, size and formation of fingers, thumb and palm, tell a story of their own, without even resorting to the lines. After studying the hands of many friends, I was asked to set up a stall in a local school fate, reading palms for a small fee. This was donated to the school funds. I dressed up as a Red Indian, calling myself "Big Heap", then spent hours servicing the queue of adults and children as they jostled for a reading.

The Length and Shape of the Thumb

The following information will present you with sufficient knowledge to get started on your quest for understanding basic human behaviour patterns through the palm. For instance, your thumb alone tells its own story by the thickness, length, and width of the nail joint in relation to the lower joint. A person with a bulbous club nail joint will show great power and determination because the top nail joint on the thumb signifies the level of will power, whilst the second joint tells the level of logic. So the difference in length and thickness of both joints in relation to each other will give an insight into the first step of basic character analysis.

For instance, you will never win an argument with a person displaying a large bulbous thumbnail joint on both hands because the will power will far exceed that person's logic. The shape of the hand itself is very revealing as a large broad hand with long square tipped fingers signifies practical ability, and a talent for paying attention to very small details. A much smaller hand with short pointed fingers shows a person who delegates, whilst overseeing the general pattern. Well-padded hands and fingers signify a vast amount of sexual energy, and slim hands with long fingers, often point to a sensitive or psychic person. There are all kinds of variations to the above information which can be analysed in far greater detail, but I have set out a very simple system for the student of psychology to study.

The Length and Shape of Fingers

The length and shape of fingers tell another story. For instance, the middle finger is usually the longest on most hands, but if the index finger is extra long and is approximately the same size as the middle finger, you are in the presence of a person who likes to dominate. The ring finger indicates a talent for histrionics or show business, so when this finger is longer than the index finger, and has a spatulate appearance, you have the urge to perform in front of an audience, which is a typical show business sign. Then the little finger is also a great give-away because if it is straight so is the person's character, but if it curves inward, you are in the presence of Foxy Loxy indicating a cunning devious mind. You will find a great variety of interesting hands to study which will take you much further into the finer details. It does take a life-time of study to be become really proficient in the art of reading a person's psychological nature through palmistry. However, it is still worthwhile to learn the basics and to have a working knowledge of the art.

The Life Line

I started studying palmistry way back in the 1960's, by reading every book on the subject that I could find. I learned that a certain number of lines on the hand identified a person's possible longevity. Firstly, from what is called a lifeline which runs in a half-circle around the thumb. A thick line, of long length, and solidarity tell of a strong constitution. But if the line shows a definite break, it means the subject will experience some form of illness at the time indicated. If the line is full of dots, chains, or island formations then that person will experience many different health problems.

The Line of Mentality

The line of mentality starts between the thumb and forefinger, sometimes joined to the lifeline, or occasionally it starts with a gap just above the lifeline, which means that the subject is more adventurous. If it extends right across the palm in a straight line, that person will be very practical. When it curves down on to the heel of the hand, which is called the mount of Moon, that subject will exhibit great imagination, and when the line splits into two sections as it curves downward, then that person's imagination will increase even further. Many creative artists, composers and writers will exhibit this particular characteristic. Once again, the formation of the line tells a parallel story. A strong powerful line will promote mental stability, and a practical approach to life. Any person with islands, breaks, or chain formations may suffer from nervous exhaustion, or exhibit some type of mental problems during their life.

The Line of Heart

The line of heart starts right above the line of mentality, either joined together, slightly above, or occasionally it starts right underneath the index finger, curves down and progresses in a straight line across the palm. Very occasionally you will come across a single combined head and heart line running straight across the palm, which is called a simian line. I have only encountered this line four times in thirty years, and it signifies great determination. A powerful strong heart line indicates a healthy emotional nature, and a strong powerful heart. Any island formations, breaks or chains will indicate an unstable emotional nature, and it often indicates problems with the arterial system, such as a high level of cholesterol, high blood pressure, and possibly a general closing up of the arterial system.

The Girdle of Venus

This line runs in a semi circle, curving upwards above the heart line, covering the two middle fingers. Not too many people are blessed with the significance of this line which indicates great sensitivity, and is often seen on the hands of musicians. In fact my father, who was a violinist, had the most perfect girdle of Venus that I have ever seen. Any child displaying this line will undoubtedly have latent musical or artistic talent.

Line of Destiny

This line runs from low down the palm, near the wrist, and often travels right up to the middle finger. When strong and clear, it indicates great success for the person in question. Breaks in the line indicate many changes of interest and occupation. If the line splits into numerous sections, that person will have many different jobs, and will rarely follow one trade or occupation.

Line of Sun

This line runs up under the ring finger, and if straight and strong, indicates possible success in life within the chosen field. It often reflects the line of destiny so that when both line of Sun and Destiny are strong and clear that person will show great determination and success in pursuing a chosen area of work. There are many other minor lines that tell other stories. Some doctors take a look at a patient's nails when you enter their surgery which is almost a subject in its own right. The fingerprints, skin ridge formations, circles, squares, dots and crosses, all tell a story.

The object of this chapter is not to present a complete picture of palmistry, which would take as many words as a full-scale book, but to indicate to the sceptics that, once again, there are more things in heaven and earth than are dreamt of by the majority of people in this "Multi Dimensional Universe."

Astrology

It is always very interesting to listen to the arguments of the sceptics because, with one accord I have never read one single paper or publication where a person has set out to do a scientific analysis, then published the results that indicate why they found that astrology does not work. The reason is very simple; there have been hundreds of thousands of articles, papers and books detailing out the basic principles, showing the correlation between the planets, stars and human behaviour, but sceptics have never taken the trouble to read, digest, test, and then analyse the results. Any person who has read Llewellyn George's A to Z horoscope maker and delineator, which was written before the first world war, and has probably been printed world-wide in hundreds of editions, may agree that it is undoubtedly the finest work of reference that has ever been published. After a prolonged study of this book, you will have stepped on the first rung of the ladder leading into the halls of Knowledge. Listen to the sceptics and ask these questions: "How do you know astrology does not work? From where did you get your information? How long have you been studying the subject? How many charts have you erected? Have you ever found that no correlation existed between the planets positions and the behaviour pattern of the Subject?" No sceptic can answer those questions.

Who Started Astrology?

The earliest recorded practitioner of astrology was a man called **Seth**, who lived about six thousand years ago when astronomy and astrology were one and the same. The study of planets was a practical down-to-earth affair, essential for navigation, judging the seasons, and weather information for planning everyday life. Seth studied the movement of the planets, and was consulted by many ancient people. The next recorded astrologer was *Enoch,* who lived about five hundred years after Seth, who also studied the planets in relation to the zodiac. Then came the Priests of Chaldea who were skilled astronomers, and they identified the five visible planets of Mercury, Venus, Mars, Jupiter and Saturn. *The Chaldean priests* studied cycles based on the figure seven, due to those five planets, plus the Sun and Moon, well before the discovery of Uranus, Neptune and Pluto. The Chaldeans decided that each day of the week was ruled by a certain planet, such as Monday ruled by the Moon, Tuesday ruled by Mars, Wednesday ruled by Mercury, Thursday ruled by Jupiter, Friday ruled by Venus, Saturday ruled by Saturn, and Sunday ruled by the Sun. The Greek mathematician *Pythagoras* who discovered geometry, was also a skilled astronomer and astrologer, and also invented an ingenious theory to explain eclipses. Another Greek called *Hipparchus,* who lived around 125 BC, made a catalogue to show the size and brightness of the stars. Probably the most famous of the Greek astrologers was *Claudius Ptolomy,* who wrote a magnificent work called the "Tetrabiblos," which has always been used as an astrological Bible. Ptolomy was one of the original great thinkers and teachers of astrology. The Arabs produced some of the world's greatest mathematicians, and around 1,000 AD, they invented our present-day numeral system. There is an Arab manuscript entitled "Elements of the Art of Astrology," by *Al Biruni,* and only one hundred translations were ever printed, so it is a very rare and prized publication. *Nicolaus Copernicus,* born in Poland in 1743, was a mathematician, scientist, astronomer, doctor and astrologer, who wrote and published many books on astronomy and astrology.

France produced one of the most famous astrologers, namely *Nostradamus* who was born in 1503. In order to prevent the church burning him as a heretic, he disguised his predictions in a series of four-line verses, or quatrains, which are now available after being translated into many different languages. He predicted that 1999 would be the year of judgment. Interestingly, on August 11th 1999 the great eclipse of the Sun heralded very destructive planetary oppositions and square aspects. This could mean that events on or around that time could manifest at some future date, bringing a vast upheaval when the planets adversely aspect that area. Possibly the greatest scientist and astrologer was *Johann Kepler,* born in 1571, who in 1594 became Professor of Mathematics at the University of Gratz, Austria. Four years later he was sacked from his post because religious bigotry interfered with his work. Later he became imperial mathematician to the Emperor Rudolph in Prague. Now here is a very interesting point because if you look up the history books, you will find that references to astrology studied by many of these great scientists was removed, and only half their work recognized. Kepler compiled a diary of his life, noting the planetary configurations, and found out after many years research that he had proved beyond reasonable doubt that human behaviour is indelibly linked up to the planetary positions, through zodiac sign, angle, aspect and house. *Galileo Galilei* was born in Pisa, Italy, and became professor of mathematics, scientist, astrologer and inventor, and on January 7th 1610 became the first man to identify the four Moons of Jupiter. Later he fell foul of the church and was forced to renounce many of his discoveries on pain of torture and death.

During the Middle Ages, England's most famous astrologer was *William Lilley,* who wrote books, sent out leaflets, and made amazing predictions based on astrology, which later proved to be very accurate. He predicted that Charles the first would lose both his throne and his head. He also predicted the great fire of London would occur in 1666. Later he was commanded to appear before Parliament to prove the accuracy of his predictions, because the authorities thought that he had started the fire! Fortunately, he was able to convince his accusers that he was innocent of causing the fire, explaining exactly how he had come to his conclusions by the positions of the planets and fixed stars in relation to the sign and degree ruling the city of London which is seventeen degrees and fifty-four minutes of Gemini. This I have personally found to be very accurate in assessing events relating to London. So on that basis, when Uranus reached the 17th degree of Sagittarius, in direct opposition to the degree ruling London, on February 22nd 1985, the pound fell to a record low in relation to the dollar of $1.0765. Interest rates were 14%, and the pound was devalued by 27%. Using this system, I was able to predict the largest one-day stock market fall in the Twentieth Century - a drop of over fifty billion pounds was wiped out on October 19th 1987 when Saturn reached the 17th degree of Sagittarius, in opposition to the degree ruling the city of London. When I was a boy, we were informed that *Sir Isaac Newton* discovered the law of gravity and invented calculus. There was no mention of astrology, or the fact that Newton spent fifteen years looking for the philosopher's stone, which legend stated that lead could be turned into gold. He never found the answer, but he became very proficient in the study of astrology, and to quote once again his answer when a learned scientist at the Royal Society derided him for being involved with astrology, claiming that it was a figment of the imagination, Newton stood up and said, *"Sir I have studied the subject and you have not."* He then sat down because there is no answer to that statement. No person can denounce any subject from a position of ignorance and no paper or publication has ever been written in the history of the human race that detailed the planetary positions at the birth of a child, and then found that there was no correlation between the planetary positions and the events that occurred during that person's life. The public are often fooled by what is called newspaper astrology, where you look up your birth sign then read your daily or monthly predictions. The system commonly used is to erect a chart placing the zodiac sign of the day or month on the ascendant, which is the eastern horizon. Then list the planets, angles, and houses from that point. This gives a false impression regarding the area of influence, so if you were not born at sunrise, or have no group of planets on, or near, the ascendant at birth, the predictions would be based mainly on chance. This gives the public a completely false impression of the validity of true astrology because using these principles any person could make a prediction, and it would by the law of averages be right for some people. Now take a look at the real principles of astrology!

The Real Principles of Astrology

The heavens are divided into twelve sections called the zodiac, through which the planets travel. The Earth is also divided into twelve sections called houses that continuously revolve due to the rotation of the earth in relation to the zodiac. This causes every sign to rise up over the Ascendant, i.e., (eastern horizon) every twenty-four hours. Your rising sign and ascending degree have influence over your health and personality, and any planet found on or near this point will considerably affect your life. The position of the Sun by sign, house and degree will pinpoint your individuality, or the real you, that only emerges during a crisis. Your Midheaven, the highest point in your chart, indicates the way that you approach your career or occupation. If you were born on or near midday, your Sun would be joined to your Midheaven, and if you were born at sunrise, your Sun would conjunct your Ascendant. By combining only these three main areas in your chart, the multiplied sum of twelve Sun Signs, twelve Ascendant Signs, and twelve Midheaven signs, throws up a total of 1,728 different Zodiac types. The degree on the eastern horizon changes approximately every four minutes, and when all the planets are introduced into the Zodiac Circle, each one multiplying the previous total by twelve the final figure reaches a staggering sum amounting to billions making every living person on planet Earth Astrologically Different. Just like the simple diagnosis in palmistry, where the shape and size of fingers and hands tell their own story, astrology also has a very simple diagnostic tool for a basic psychological analysis, which is the distribution of the four elements.

Fire, Earth, Air and Water

1. Aries, Leo and Sagittarius are the fire signs, indicating the element of action. This group never let grass grow under their feet.
2. Taurus, Virgo and Capricorn are the earth signs, indicating a much more cautious and practical approach to life and business.
3. Gemini, Libra and Aquarius are the air signs, and have great ability to communicate through writing, art and music.
4. Cancer, Scorpio and Pisces are water signs, and are the most sensitive and psychic people, and are often found in the medical or healing business.

Fire signs are most compatible with other fire signs. Earth signs with other earth signs. Air signs with other air signs, and water signs with other water signs. Then there are the following three designations, which also slot into place also telling their own story.

Cardinal, Fixed and Mutable

The cardinal signs are *Aries, Cancer, Libra and Capricorn*, indicating a combination of power and flexibility.

The fixed signs of **Taurus, Leo, Scorpio and Aquarius** are immovable in their approach to life, and have great difficulty in changing direction.

The mutable signs, **Gemini, Virgo, Sagittarius and Pisces** have much more flexibility than the other designations.

Regardless of your Sun sign, if you have the majority of planets in fixed signs, you will never bend with the wind, and you never give way because yours is the only opinion that matters. If the majority of planets are in mutable signs, you will be capable of changing direction in life without too much trouble. The cardinal signs are a combination of the previous two designations with the power of the fixed signs, and the flexibility of the mutable signs. Check these designations by looking up your friends and family to see how their basic psychological characteristics fit in with the above information.

Success in Life

Your basic success pattern in life often depends where Jupiter designated the great planet of luck and abundance was placed, by the sign, house, and the angles it makes to any other planets at birth. One of the most potent aspects for success is a sixty, or one-hundred-and-twenty degree angle between Jupiter and your Natal Sun, or a conjunction of Sun and Jupiter at birth, which will result in more than your fair share of opportunities to become rich and famous. Also a group of planets in any one sign will channel energy through that area for better or worse, depending on the aspects of the remaining planets.

1. Jupiter aspecting your Sun means great success in your chosen field of endeavour.

2. Jupiter to Moon means success with in the Fashion World, Dealing with the Public, Antiques, Liquids and all Dairy Products.

3. Jupiter to Mercury means success with Writing, Publishing, Printing, Advertising, Lecturing, The Law, and Transport.

4. Jupiter to Venus means success in the Art World, Music, Fashion, Photography and Painting.

5. **Jupiter to Mars** means success in Athletics Sporting events of all kinds, including the Armed Forces.

6. **Jupiter to Uranus** covers success with Computers, Electronics, and gain from Premium Bonds.

7. **Jupiter to Saturn** means gain from Property, Building Projects, and the Business World.

8. **Jupiter to Neptune** pinpoints success in Show Business, Music, Photography, Shipping, Fishing, Brewing and Chemicals.

9. **Jupiter to Pluto** points to success as a Detective, Surgeon, Police, Mining, Oil and Insurance.

Your Natal Astrology Chart

Your natal chart is calculated from your time, date and place of birth, pinpointing longitude and latitude, enabling us to indicate your rising sign, and all your planets down to the exact degree. Then by showing your beneficial and difficult aspects, you can plan your life with greater confidence, knowing that you can be successful in certain areas, pinpointed by your planetary positions.

Great Financial Success

For instance, most millionaires are easily identified by their planetary groupings and aspects at birth. A conjunction of Sun, Jupiter and Venus in any sign, situated in a person's second house, without any adverse aspects, will always indicate great financial success. When I have been involved with after-dinner speeches on astrology, I always ask for about a dozen people to write out their date of birth, and place the results in a hat. Then during the talk I usually pick out a few at random, then slap a ruler under that exact date, using a large ephemeris, and have a quick look at the groupings and angles of the planets for that day. This takes about sixty seconds to do a rough check, and then decide what that person does for a living. This information is obtained by checking the strength and groupings of the planets not the zodiac signs then deciding what is the strongest area. There are certain areas in the zodiac circle that pinpoint and increase lifetime. But if a major aspect is indicated, it will last for about three years, for better or worse, depending how it aspects your natal and other progressed planets. Mercury, Venus, Mars, Jupiter and Saturn, all contribute to the heavenly progressed dance. However, the outer planets move very slowly by progression, so they may never make an aspect during your lifetime.

The Transiting Planets

When the major progressed planets make an aspect, they are influenced by the transiting planets circling above. The slow-moving outer planets such as Pluto, Neptune and Uranus will change your life completely if they ever make a major aspect to any natal planet. Pluto will bring the greatest change in your life, if it ever makes a major conjunction with your natal Sun or Moon. Neptune works its magic by opening up your consciousness and increases your psychic faculties. It can also bring success in show business and music. Uranus brings sudden success or shocks, depending on its position at birth, and Saturn the great planet of fate, joins your Sun approximately every twenty-nine years. Jupiter takes twelve years to circle the zodiac, bringing luck and abundance whenever it activates a benefic planetary configuration in your natal or progressed chart. The other transiting planets Mars, Venus, Mercury and also the Moon, act as triggers to set in motion the major events in your life. Not quite so simple as the sceptics make out?

Astrologically, I have a number of very good aspects at birth, with the Sun in Virgo in the fifth house of my astrology chart in brilliant aspect to the Moon, Saturn, Mercury and Pluto. This is probably why I have obtained over one hundred wins on football pools, eight wins on premium bonds, numerous wins on the lottery, though the highest was around £111. I have also picked two seven-horse accumulators, and one six-horse accumulator, althoughthe jackpot has yet to be won. As Shakespeare wrote, *"There is a tide in the affairs of men which taken at the flood leads on to fortune."*

If you can pinpoint the area of gain within your astrology chart, and then wait for the planets to slot into place, you will undoubtedly benefit financially. For instance, in 1968, 1969 and 1970 there was a great astrological influence on my fifth house, ruling gambling, speculation and children. My progressed Moon, Jupiter, Uranus and Pluto, all crossed my natal Sun, indicating a sudden shock, change of direction, and a possible upturn financially. This grouping of planets angled my natal Saturn and Moon, activating the grand trine in my chart. My father was born under the sign of Aquarius, so his ruling planet was Uranus. My Midheaven is also Aquarius, so when Mercury, my ruling planet, and Venus made a conjunction to my Midheaven, at eighteen degrees Aquarius, Pluto joined my natal Mercury, and on March 6th 1968 Uranus reached the exact conjunction of my natal Sun, at twenty-seven degrees and forty minutes Virgo. On that very same day, my father passed from this world to the next. The sceptics would say that it was a coincidence, but there is more to follow. With Pluto, Jupiter and my progressed Moon travelling through my zodiac sign of Virgo, also activating the grand trine in my birth chart, I wrote and published three books, which made a considerable amount of money. When Pluto made an exact conjunction with my natal Sun in December 1969, Robert my son was born. Uranus at the same time was also exactly conjunct his mother's natal Sun-Mercury aspect, making those three years the most emotionally evoking, yet financially rewarding, and prolific time of my life. How strange that this successful period was exactly pinpointed by the planetary aspects in the heavens. Could this be just a coincidence? Or does astrology really work?

A Basic Stock Market Prediction

When the last big London stock market crash occurred, and the price of property also dropped, The Daily Express continuously reported, possibly hundreds of times that the property market was on the way up. Yet there was no evidence that this rise was happening. Why? What interest would that newspaper have in promoting the property market? At the end of August 2006, there was an opposition of Saturn from 17 degrees Leo to Neptune at 17 degrees Aquarius. This combination covers business in general, show business, gambling, speculation, shipping, fishing, brewing, aviation, and the electronics industry. There could be considerable changes in any business connected with these industries. At the end of September 2006 Jupiter adversely aspected Neptune promoting a vast illusion with the National Health Service. Mercury, Venus and Mars opposes the degree ruling the London Stock Market in December 2006, so there could be far less spent by the public at Christmas which will echo through the markets in 2007. With Jupiter, Venus, Uranus and the Moon's nodes adverse to London, there are likely to be considerable fluctuations in the business and property markets in February 2007. This will be followed by a few very nasty shocks at the end of April and early May 2007 when the stock market could take a beating. This volatile trend will undoubtedly continue right through 2007 because we have all been living under a false illusion for too may years. So, batten down the hatches, hold on to your money and wait for better times before investing. This publication will be followed by a new book on astrology, using a slightly different system, which will help people to pinpoint the possible rise and fall of the stock market. It will also help readers to understand the psychological relationship within a family unit.

The Tarot

The next area of controversy is tarot cards, which have been in existence since the Middle Ages, though no one actually knows where they originally came from or who painted the original designs. One of the finest books on the tarot is written by Alfred Douglas, or Bosie as his friends call him. He is married to Jo Sheridan, and both used to write a column for Prediction Magazine in the days when Madeline Montalban wrote the most enlightened articles on the metaphysical world that I have ever read. The Tarot is not just a fortune telling system which can be used by psychics to focus on future events. It was originally designed to teach self-realization, by taking a student through twenty-two different stages of development leading to the ultimate level of enlightenment. This is indicated by card number twenty-one, "The World." There are seventy-eight cards in the tarot pack, comprising twenty-two picture cards called the major arcane, and fifty-six cards in the minor arcane. Most readers use the full pack, but I personally have always used only the picture cards of the major arcane. Each student must experiment and find what works for them.

My Personal System

For instance, I shuffle the cards for a couple of minutes while concentrating on the question in mind. Then I cut the cards and lay the first one down on my left, placing each one in turn straight off the top of the pack anti clockwise, until twelve cards are laid out in a circle, with the thirteenth card in the centre. This last card is the key to the layout because it influences all the other cards in the circle. To use this method you will need to understand the house system in astrology because the first card signifies your personality, health, and how you communicate on a one-to-one basis. The second card, or second house in astrology, relates to your money and financial affairs. The third card covers transport, writings and short distance travel. The fourth card covers your property, and everything that happens within your home. The fifth card covers romance, gambling speculation and children. The sixth card pinpoints your health, and your work, but not your career, which is covered by a different area. The seventh card covers marriage and partnerships, also open enemies. The eighth card covers insurance and investments of all kinds. The ninth card pinpoints publishing, higher education, overseas travel, and all legal problems. The tenth card covers your career and business interests. The eleventh card covers friends of all types. The twelfth card covers all your personal secrets, and secret enemies. This means that any card slotting into a specific house will indicate exactly what is happening at the moment in time that the question is asked. For instance, if the wheel of fortune falls into your fifth house of gambling and speculation you could win with games of chance providing that you have no adverse fifth house astrological aspects at birth. If the death card, the lightning struck tower, or the fool appears in your fifth house then under no circumstances speculate or gamble because you will probably lose. The following twenty-two cards in the Major Arcane are listed below, with a very basic meaning for each card.

"Card number 0 is the Fool" Signifying that you must take extra care in the area that it falls, for instance if it falls in your second house, it would signify that you should take a second look at any business or proposition connected with finance because impulsive action could bring serious financial problems.

"Card number 1 is the "Magician" Signifying the ability to juggle events to suit yourself, so if it falls into your second house of finance, you will have many options to choose from. You have great self-confidence, and a willingness to take financial risks.

"Card number 2 is the "High Priestess" Signifying the intuitive influence of a powerful woman, linking the physical/spiritual worlds, helping to open your subconscious mind to the reality of nature

"Card number 3 is the "Empress" Signifying the impact of motherhood, success, and stability in home life, security and growth for the future.

"Card number 4 is the "Emperor" Great authority, with creative power and energy, directed towards a successful conclusion in any area that this card falls.

"Card number 5 is the "Hierophant or Pope" Wisdom and enlightenment can be received through spiritual insight, and also that which is hidden can be brought out in to the open.

"Card number 6 is the "Lovers" Does not denote physical love, unless it falls into the fifth house of romance and children, where it means that a love affair is on the way. Covers initiative and personal progress by your own efforts, and success through long-term projects which you really love doing.

"Card number 7 is the "Chariot" This card signifies a battle fought and a battle won by successfully climbing over many obstacles. If it falls in your eighth house of insurance, inheritance and investment, you should benefit in that area.

"Card number 8 is "Justice" This card returns to you all that you have given out, with words and deeds, so if you are in business, and it falls in the tenth house ruling your career, you can be successful if you have set your business up with great care; but if you have jumped in head-first you are likely to feel great repercussions in the future.

"Card number 9 is the "Hermit" This card shows an old man with a lantern pointing the way, so where this card falls, look carefully at the house position. If it falls in your sixth house of health, check your weight and cholesterol.

"Card number 10 is the "Wheel of Fortune" Meaning that fortune is on its way, through the area and house in which it falls. For instance, if you are a writer, and the wheel drops into your ninth house ruling publishing, or your third house ruling transport and communications, then the omens for success are very bright.

"Card number 11 is "Strength" This card signifies power and fortitude in the face of adversity, and your ability to conquer inner fear.

"Card number 12 is " The Hanging Man" This card means that for the time being, you will find yourself in a state of suspended animation, balancing between the world of matter and the world of spirit.

"Card number 13 is "Death" This card does not mean physical death, it simply means that you are in for a great change. If it falls in your eleventh house ruling friends, you will probably have difficulties with a specific friend. If it falls in the seventh house of partnerships and marriage, there will be considerable changes in a business partnership or marital relationship.

"Card number 14 is "Temperance" Success comes by carefully checking all the facts and then weighing up all possibilities before committing yourself to any form of action.

"Card number 15 is the "Devil" This card indicates trouble, and great changes in any area it falls. If it falls in your sixth house indicating your health and well being, you may be overdoing it with too much work.

"Card number 16 is the "Tower" If the tower falls in any area of the circle it means that you are in for a shock. For instance if it falls in your second house of finance, you will probably receive a very large bill that you were not expecting, and if it falls in your fourth house, indicating your home life; take extra precautions against accidents or burglars; check and double your security.

"Card number 17 is the "Star" Signifying a new beginning and change of circumstances, which will give great improvement in any area that it falls.

"Card number 18 is the "Moon" This card has a different meaning to the Moon in astrology. Here it signifies deceit and treachery, so if it falls in your twelfth house of secrets and secret enemies, you may find that you are under a vitriolic psychic attack from a person that you consider friendly.

"Card number 19 is the "Sun" This card is just the opposite of the Moon, and will bring a cheerful happy event into your life, also great success especially if it falls into your fifth house of romance, covering children and speculation.

"Card number 20 is "Judgment" Judge not others lest ye be judged yourself. This card signifies that if you are brought into a court of law for an offence and the card falls into your ninth house, you will receive a perfect judgment depending on what you have accomplished.

"Card number 21 is "The World" This is the card that signifies great success in any area that it lands. Study the house system carefully, and you will find that it depicts an accurate assessment of where you are going. For instance, if you are planning to buy a new or second hand car and the World falls into your third house of transport and communications then that is a very beneficial time to buy your new car.

These twenty-two cards, when used with the combined astrology house system, will start you on a path of learning because each card is a gateway to another dimension, and will show you what is in operation within your subconscious mind at any given time. The information regarding the twenty-two cards is very basic. A further study must be undertaken to extend your knowledge. However, by using my simple system, you can start your journey which will eventually enlighten your life, and help to free you from all forms of religious and political bigotry.

Chapter Sixteen
Eclipse: The Greatest Racehorse that Ever Lived

The greatest racehorse that ever lived was bred by the Duke of Cumberland and named "Eclipse" because it was born at the time of a total solar eclipse on April 1st 1764. It was then purchased by William Wildman who later sold a half-share to Col. Dennis O'Kelly. The chestnut horse stood over sixteen hands high, and when he won his first race in 1769 whilst carrying twelve stone in weight, the heaviest ever carried by a winner of the handicap, he went on to reach the stars in racing history. Eclipse never lost, and after half-a-dozen races, the betting was not whether he would win but by how many lengths he would finish in front of the other horses. He made a fortune for his owners, and remained unbeaten until he retired after eighteen races.

When he eventually galloped into the world of spirit, scientists and medics for years attempted to analyse why this horse could run so fast, and after a complete autopsy, the only real conclusion was that he had a very large heart. They dissected and analysed every inch of the muscles and bony structure, and still could not find the real reason for his great success. Thirty years ago I read an article about this magnificent creature, and recently Sharon Wright once again brought this amazing feat to light in the Daily Express. To the best of my knowledge, no scientist or medic has the faintest idea why this horse was so successful on the racetrack. However, I can tell you why. After studying Astrology for over thirty years, I have analysed the planetary positions at the time of birth. Even before I checked, I would have bet my shirt that Jupiter, the great planet of abundance, was making either a sixty-degree sextile angle, or a one-hundred-and-twenty-degree trine angle, from the eclipse at the time of birth. The eclipse occurred in the 12th degree of Aries, conjunct the fixed star Alpheratz, which is a double white star, formally located in Pegasus, the winged horse of mythology. How about that for a coincidence? Its influence according to Ptolemy is of the nature of both Venus and Jupiter combined, and joined to the Sun gives honour and success. With the Moon conjunction it gives great energy, honour, wealth, and business success. With Uranus at 16 degrees Aries, conjunct the eclipse by only four degrees adding genius, magic, and sudden great success. Can there have ever been a more significant categorization of an event, using astrology and mythology combined? So what would the sceptics make of such an amazing coincidence? ***Of all the stars in the heavens, this horse was born, not only at the time of an eclipse of the Sun, but in the area of sky that links up with the mythical winged horse Pegasus.***

The great Swiss psychologist Carl Jung taught the meaning of synchronicity, and this has to be one of the ultimate indications of his beliefs. Any birth that comes into being at the time of a solar eclipse will have great significance for success or failure, depending of course on the other planetary positions at the time of birth, regardless of whether it is human, animal or mechanical. All things are governed by the moment in time of their birth, but within that cycle we can influence future events depending on the spirituality of the people concerned. Jupiter the great planet of luck and abundance was situated in the 12th degree of Gemini, making an exact 60-degree sextile aspect to the eclipse. It was also flanked by two category one fixed stars, Rigel and Aldebaron, indicating a combined influence of Jupiter and Mars which in any chart signifies great success in life, for that person, or horse on this occasion.

Mars, ruler of Aries, was in the 13th degree of Sagittarius, throwing a fantastic 120-degree trine aspect to the eclipse indicating great athletic ability. All other aspects are totally insignificant in relation to this magnificent combination. Any person born at the same time would have been a great athlete, and would have become very rich and famous. I wonder whether there is any record of a human birth at the time of the eclipse because it would be very interesting to compare the overall life-style of horse and human. Aries is the all-action, cardinal fire sign of the zodiac, with Mars ruling and the second decan between the 10th to 20th degrees of Aries sub-ruled by Leo, a fixed fire sign, so that the Sun as ruler of Leo throws an extra fiery energy into the pot. Having no record of exactly where the horse was born, my chart for the eclipse was erected at Manchester. We have the time but not the place, so within a hundred miles or so in the north of England, the planets would be in exactly that same place at the time of birth, with only the ascendant Midheaven and the house cusps slightly different. However, I have placed the ascendant at 16 degrees Cancer. This second decan of Cancer is sub-ruled by Scorpio bringing extra power and strength, and what a coincidence! This is exactly where the part of fortune is situated for this location at the time of birth. The Midheaven is 13 degrees Pisces, sub-ruled by Cancer, so the water signs are prominent in the combination of Ascendant and Midheaven. This would signify that the arterial and lymphatic system of the horse would be very well developed and work magnificently.

The Eclipse, Uranus, the north node of the Moon and Mercury, is situated in the tenth house, and as every astrologer knows, influences the career of the person or horse concerned, for good or bad, depending on the aspects, so that any person with this combination would undoubtedly end up with millions in the bank. Also the horse made a vast fortune for its owners. The four elements of fire, earth, air and water are dominated by the all-action fire element of Mars.

Saturn is situated in 7th degree of Taurus, throwing a great 120-degree trine aspect to Pluto in 5th degree of Capricorn. This aspect in earth signs points to brilliant business success in all things ruled by those two planets, so the owners could have invested in property and mining shares, and succeeded very well. Venus is in the 18th degree of Taurus, throwing a close 60-degree sextile aspect to Mercury in 12th degree of Pisces. Note Mercury is in the tenth house ruling career, and Libra is on the cusp of the fifth house of gambling, speculation and any sporting event, including horse racing. Once again we have another link to success within this area.

The last remaining planet Neptune, is situated in 26th degrees of Leo, and is not far off a grand trine with Saturn and Pluto and, as most astrologers know, a grand trine of three planets all operating within a range of 120 degrees from each other creating a triangle is one of the most powerful aspects for success in any person's chart. The only really difficult aspect in this chart is the opposition from Jupiter in 12th degree of Gemini, in the twelfth house of secrets, in opposition to Mars at 13 degrees Sagittarius, in the sixth house, with Mercury forming a wide adverse T-square from the tenth house. This points to a possibility that the horse was fed with cocktails of speed-enhancing drugs, which boosted muscle power and delivered extra oxygen. The give-away is that when the surgeons performed an autopsy, they discovered that Eclipse had a very unusual enlarged heart, and that is one of the symptoms of a certain type of steroid drugs, which may or may not have been known during the eighteenth century. In those times, I expect every horse was doctored with some type of drug, and Eclipse turned out to be the ultimate winner of all time.

A possible System for Beating the Bookmakers

I have always been interested in horse racing, and I have found a simple formula for winning. I happen to have a very good grouping of planets in my fifth house at birth, ruling speculation, gambling, children and show business. So when this area in my natal chart is activated, I can plan my attack on local bookmakers. I am not a compulsive gambler so I only make a bet three or four times each year.

The Value of Checking Birth dates

I begin by looking up the birthdays of any top jockey and trainer because they are more likely to win on or around their birth date. The next step is to check the planetary positions for the day in question, and if the Sun and Moon are in good aspect, for instance, making a 60 degree sextile aspect, or a 120 degree trine aspect. On that day the majority of favourites should win. So an accumulator, picking out the most likely horses with the very lowest odds should give you a financial return. However, if you do not have a gambler's chart in the first place, you are unlikely ever to beat the bookies. I have one astrology client that has commissioned me to erect his chart every year for the last twenty-five years. He was born with a gambler's chart, so I work out his best months of the year from the influences of the major planetary positions in relation to his natal chart, and then pinpoint the best position of the Moon each month. Since the Moon moves approximately half a degree per hour, I select the best two-hour cycle within that framework. In some circumstances, I found that I could narrow the time down to a period of sixteen minutes due to the rotation of the earth in relation to his major natal progressions and transiting planets, occasionally bringing spectacular results. I have never met this man face-to-face, and have only spoken to him by phone twice in twenty five years, but as he keeps coming back for more information every year, I gather he is using my predictions to help beat the system.

Chapter Seventeen
Organized Religion

I was brought up as a Welsh Baptist, and because my father was treasurer, deacon and choirmaster of the local Baptist chapel in Birmingham, I was taken to chapel for the morning service, then Sunday school in the afternoon, and then the evening service. I never listened to the preacher because he droned away, reading passages out of the bible, and almost sending me off to sleep, making the chapel seem more like a tomb rather than a place of worship. My father wanted me to join the Boys' Brigade marching around the district puffing bugles and beating drums, but being such an awkward devil, I joined the scouts instead. When the Boys' Brigade marched along our road, I stood on the corner sucking a lemon, so that a few unharmonious notes were belted out much to my amusement.

My main memories of scouting came from some of the nicknames given to various members of the scouting fraternity. One scout was named Austin Leek, so his nickname was Ford Onion, another friend living nearby was named Norman Coates, and his nickname was Roman Trousers. When I was fourteen years of age, I met the most beautiful blonde girl that I have ever seen and fell madly in love. She danced and sang on the stage, so religion disappeared into the background because we started going to the cinema on a Sunday evening instead of chapel. Then I completely extracted myself from the organized religion of the Baptist faith, yet my father never said one word against my diversion of interest. Both my parents were beautiful people who never said a bad word about anyone.

Religious people very much like the idea of a benevolent God giving life everlasting in a heavenly abode after death because it makes them feel secure whilst they are living on earth. But if there is a heaven or hell in another dimension, how do we qualify to enter the gates of heaven? Will we be provided with a heavenly passport if we are good, and will we be cast into a fiery hell if we are not, and who is to examine our credentials for either dimension? When any religion promises life if you do what you are told, and death everlasting if you do not follow their specific philosophy, you then know that they are using a technique of blackmail to gain control.

The great masters, responsible for starting many of the religions on this planet never intended their teachings to be violated with such controlling behaviour in the first place. They taught the Law of Karma, but we humans in our absolute stupidity cast aside the very basics of religious belief, based upon love and goodwill to all men.

To Quote the Teachings of the Buddha

Thought manifests as the word; the word manifests as the deed; the deed develops into habit. Then habit hardens into character; Watch the thought process with care. Let it develop from love, born out of concern for all living creatures. The shadow of thought then manifests into the material world. *As we think, so we become.*

Often in the past, one specific religious group regularly knocked on my door punching home their ideology. I invited them in and with one accord I found that they were unable to think for themselves. They had all been brainwashed by the system and continuously quoted passages from the bible. After much discussion, I was asked whether they could bring their boss next time they visited me. I agreed, and when he arrived, he brought along a group of people. We had a very long discussion and then the headman informed me that he could convert me to their religion in three months. "What utter arrogance." I asked him if he believed in a cunning and evil Devil? He replied, "Absolutely." I asked him how could he differentiate between God and the Devil. Which was which? He looked very startled especially when I stated that if I were the Devil, I would set up a religious order, and have millions of unsuspecting humans doing my bidding, thinking they were worshipping God. But in fact they would be worshipping the Devil.

How about that for a cunning strategy? When you think about the problems created by dominating religions, my theory may not be so far out of touch as many so-called religious people would like to believe. When the group realised that I could not be controlled by their blackmail approach, they left never to return. It is astonishing to observe their doorstep approach and the lengths to which they go in order to bombard unsuspecting people into allowing them access to their homes, and then trying to set up a fear syndrome within the psyche of the recipient.

If you look back a couple of thousand years, more people have been killed by religious fanatics in the name of their God, than all the wars put together. This has made many areas of organised religions the curse of humanity. My personal philosophy is never to let a priest or religion get between the Cosmic Creator and myself. The only way to find out the truth is through the saying. *"Do what thou will, providing it does not harm or control any other person or living creature."* This is the basic principle of the law of cause and effect, and if you observe human behaviour you will find that every action and thought will return to its source sometime during your life.

One very interesting but sad event took place well after my father died. His beloved Baptist Chapel was burnt down and to my knowledge was never rebuilt. Since living in London during the 1960's, I often attended numerous spiritual churches where a medium gave readings to the congregation. However, as a professional photographer, I have had many disputes with conventional religions regarding the taking photographs of inside a church during a wedding.

When I was twenty-one years of age, I was working for a news agency doing press photography, and one client was The Jewish Chronicle. I was asked by the editor to go up into the gallery and shoot pictures at the opening of the new Synagogue in Birmingham, by the Chief Rabbi, Dr Israel Brody. I was in total ignorance of the Jewish religion, and had no previous contact, so I climbed up the stairs and found a place in the gallery little realizing that only women were allowed in that part of the Synagogue. As the Chief Rabbi led a procession down the aisle, I leant over the balcony and let off a large flashbulb. He looked up with amazement, and then two men in top hats dashed into the gallery and literally hustled me out of the Synagogue. At the reception afterwards I apologized to the Chief Rabbi for my ignorance. He was very understanding and asked who sent me up into the women's gallery. When I told him that it was the editor of the Jewish Chronicle, he smiled and said. "I will have words with him later."

During one Church of England wedding that I photographed, the priest stated that I could take pictures on the vicarage lawn after the service, so I set up groups and proceeded to shoot the formal pictures.

Then I dashed outside into the garden to get a shot of the Bride and Groom, using the gateway to frame the picture. As I was leaving, I met the Vicar coming in, his mouth was wide open, and he was gnashing his teeth and gesticulating furiously. "They are doing it on my lawn," he screamed. I spun around with my camera at the ready not knowing what to expect only to perceive that they were being bombarded with confetti on his sacred lawn.

I once photographed a wedding at a well-known London Church of England. When I arrived, the vicar shot out of the church and made a beeline for me. He looked like the proverbial comic vicar with buckteeth, pebble glasses and a high-pitched nasal voice. "No photographs allowed in my church," he screamed. "You will stay outside the church during the ceremony, and when the register has been signed, you will come around to the back of the church then we will let you in to take one picture." As the bride and father walked down the aisle, with the Vicar in front of the procession, a woman stood up in a pew and flashed a picture. The vicar went red with rage and screamed. "No photographs in my church," then rushed towards the said lady with his hand held straight out in a Hitler style salute. "My God," I thought, "a violent vicar, what would he have done to me if I had flashed off a picture?"

Is the object of the Church of England to keep the public out because the Roman Catholic and Greek religions allow complete access for photography during a wedding ceremony, and usually have large congregations? If the Royal family can have access for photography during a wedding ceremony, why can't the British public have the same privilege? On another occasion I was in Birmingham photographing a wedding, when the Vicar approached and said, "No photographs to be taken in my church." I went into the church, and near the altar was a video cameraman setting up a tripod. I accosted the Vicar and asked him why he was allowing a video of the wedding but not a stills cameraman. He became very aggressive and stated that a video was not photography, and screamed at me once again "No photographs allowed in my church."

I wonder whether these little dictators have any idea, that this is the worst public relations that could possibly happen to any religion.

Do we really need great brick temples to worship the creator, and do we need a society of priests in fancy dress to bring us the word of God? The greatest temples are woodland areas, hills or mountain tops, rock pools near the ocean, flowing rivers and streams with dragon flies hovering over the water, swallows flying through trees, then bats flitting around at dusk as you feel a warm breeze on a summer evening whilst sitting under an oak tree. Can you think of a more spiritual place to sit and meditate? I know that there are churches and temples that vibrate the light, but how can a man-built edifice compete with the magnificent temples of nature?

The Danger of Fundamentalist Religions

One sure way to recognize any destructive element within fundamentalist religions is if they threaten violence to anyone who criticizes their philosophy; or destroy books that conflict with their religious beliefs. This is the first principle of attempting to exercise total control at a later date. Once they ban free speech then the next step is to take over the country, brainwash the majority of people, and fly their personal flag at every opportunity. Stalin and Hitler followed this principle until the Law of Karma stepped in and destroyed them both. In the end most religions will fall unless they adopt a philosophy such as that of the Cathar prophesy listed in the early chapter of this book.

Let the light of love filter through every atom of your being, then you will truly find the way and the light, which will lift you to the stars, setting you free from human domination.

Chapter Eighteen
The Philosophy of Accidents

What exactly is an accident? Is it an event that occurs suddenly without warning or is it the result of previous behaviour catching up with ourselves, such as the cause and effect law in operation, working to teach us a lesson? The great Swiss psychologist C.G. Jung was once asked what he would do if an accident occurred outside his house. He replied that he would 'look at his life very carefully indeed'. He was fully aware of the Law of Karma and so he answered accordingly. If you ignore these types of events without examining your own behaviour pattern you can be sure that further accidents will occur.

To give you an illustration, a few years ago a friend asked me for a loan of money and made no effort to return it. A few months later he asked me for more money without offering to pay back the original loan. This time I refused to play ball and turned him down. I didn't mention the original loan, neither did he, and once again he approached me for more money which I refused. At the same time he was continuously boasting about the money he earned, his overseas property, and the amount he spent on cars and holidays. Yet he made no effort to return my original loan. It appeared that he had also taken financial advantage of many local people. I felt rather sorry for him because I knew the cause and effect law would eventually start to operate.

When he was on a car journey through Europe, he was involved in a massive pile up on the motorway. His car was towed away to the police pound. He hired a vehicle to continue his journey, stopped at a roadside restaurant and, during the meal, the hired car was broken into and some of his luggage was stolen. After ascertaining the damage he hired a replacement car and continued his journey. At another stopping place the second vehicle was broken into and more items were stolen. On returning to London and entering his place of work, he was informed that his services were no longer required and he was sacked. Then six thousand pounds worth of tools were stolen from his garage. After he had replaced some of his tools, thieves once again broke into his garage and stole his remaining tools, yet he still came around to ask me for more money just before Christmas. He was then informed that his vehicle had been stolen from the police pound in Germany and a few weeks later, he was banned from driving for three years for excessive speeding. Next he fell of a motor cycle and broke his leg, his marriage broke up and he had a very severe heart attack. The reason for all his accidents is undoubtedly that he was triggering the Karmic Law against himself without the faintest idea of what he was setting in motion.

As you sow, you will reap!

It seemed that this man's consciousness was totally locked into the material plane. His focus seemed to be whatever he could obtain by any means available. So here we have a series of so called accidents triggered by a personal behaviour pattern. Apart from pressing your own self-destruction button, there are times when an event can be predicted in advance. By knowing the implications of the cause and effect law you can avoid serious harm by asking for guidance through prayer.

Another series of strange events occurred when a motor mechanic friend went off with a girl I was dating. This particular girl lived in a small flat directly opposite my apartment, while he and his wife lived on the top floor in the next block, at an angle to the opposite flat. We both overlooked her apartment which was situated two floors below. Early one morning, on looking out of my window I perceived him and the girl walking around her apartment totally naked without the curtains drawn. His own flat was even higher than mine, so his wife must have witnessed his activities. She then kicked him out of the family home. On another occasion after servicing my vehicle, I was travelling through Hackney, when the engine suddenly started coughing and stuttering. When I stopped and lifted the bonnet, one of the plugs had come unscrewed, so I screwed it back and continued my journey. Later I found out that my motor mechanic friend had used the wrong type and size of plugs, which could have ruined the engine. A few months later he set up in business and opened a new garage. This was situated underneath a multi-storey car park. There was a narrow passageway leading to his premises, with numerous businesses on either side, including a car valeting service. A new customer arrived and left his Porsche with the garage for servicing and cleaning. The valeting service was about thirty yards from his garage entrance, and the task was given to a young inexperienced person who, on entering the vehicle, put the car into gear and stamped on the accelerator. The car hurtled down the passageway, crashed through a brick wall and demolished the garage lift. This event happened just before Christmas, and when the damage was assessed, both car and lift were written off by the insurance company. Then whilst he was waiting for Father Christmas to arrive, thieves broke into his garage and stole all his tools. He did not recover financially and was forced to close up the garage. His wife then divorced him. It is arguable that the law of cause and effect was undoubtedly in operation during that period in his life. It is often easy to predict the reason for a person's business and health problems, once you apply the Law of Karma to their behaviour pattern.

Years ago, I knew a family with four children. The wife died when the eldest daughter was fourteen years of age. She became mother, looked after the house, and also worked in the family fish and chip shops, whilst the father pursued other business interests. After a couple of years the father met and later married a woman one year older than the eldest daughter. An interesting point to mention is that the new wife was friendly with a specific woman that I knew, who later told me that when her friend entered the father's business premises at Christmas, and observed a large cash turnover with thousands of pounds littered all over the office floor, her eyes stood out like organ stops, and her exact words were: *"My God, I have never seen so much money."* Two years later they were married. The years rolled by, and the new wife managed to stash away a considerable amount of money, but the four children from the father's previous marriage were left to fend for themselves. Eventually the son left his father's business to work in a factory in order to earn more money. After a while the father did everything possible to bring his son back into the fold, and even produced his will showing him that he would one day inherit the family business and become a rich man. The prodigal son was then welcomed back into the fold, little realising what was in store when the father eventually died.

After his passing, the family gathered in the solicitor's office to hear the terms of the will. The children were utterly shocked because the will had been changed with the stepmother receiving every penny, including the business that had been promised to the son. The grandchildren were left not one single farthing. When the solicitor was reading the will, he lowered his eyes, never looking any one of them in the face, so I suggested that they checked the date when the second will was written, and the validity of the signature. Unfortunately my suggestion fell on deaf ears.

Wills Can Be Forged

When a distant relative with a lucrative business died leaving no will, the eldest son asked his brother and sister what they wanted from the estate. They came to an agreement and, being an engraver by trade he was able to write out the will to everyone's satisfaction, forge his father's signature, and no one was ever the wiser. If this event could go undetected by law, who is to say whether the will mentioned above was not forged, just before the father died, or even after he had passed away. In that situation, the son continued to run the business. However, he was now working for his stepmother and she was now having an affair with a member of the staff. One day, lover-boy fell down a flight of stairs and broke his neck.

Did he fall or was he pushed? All the staff thought that the old man had returned from the dead then pushed him down the stairs. After a period of time, the son asked his stepmother whether he could buy the business and offered her a fair price. Before a deal could be finalized, she sold it over his head to another person. Once again he was left with nothing from all the years that he had slaved in his father's business. After a short illness the stepmother died very young, leaving all the family money to her own daughter. I would prefer never to acquire money in this manner because who knows what is waiting for the recipient who eventually collects all the family money.

Chapter Nineteen
Strange Coincidences

How do you explain the following event which can only be described as unbelievable, except that it is true, and was sent to me by email? Abraham Lincoln was elected to congress in 1846. John F. Kennedy was elected to congress one hundred years later in 1946. Abraham Lincoln was elected president in 1860. One hundred years later John F. Kennedy was elected president in 1960. Both were champions of the civil rights movements. Both lost children when in office at the White House. Both presidents were shot in the head on a Friday. Lincoln's secretary was named Kennedy, and Kennedy's secretary was named Lincoln. Men from the Deep South assassinated both, and both were succeeded by men from the south with the same name, even though the events took place one hundred years apart. Andrew Johnson who succeeded Lincoln was born in 1808. Lyndon Johnson who succeeded Kennedy was born in 1908. John Wilkes Booth who assassinated Lincoln was born in 1839. Lee Harvey Oswald who assassinated Kennedy was born in 1939. Both assassins were known by their three names, and both names comprised fifteen letters. Lincoln was shot in a theatre named Ford. Kennedy was shot in a Lincoln car made by Ford. Lincoln was shot in a theatre, and his assassin hid in a warehouse. Kennedy was shot from a warehouse, and his assassin hid in a theatre. Both assassins were themselves assassinated before they could be brought to trial. A week before Lincoln was shot he was visiting a place called Monroe in Maryland. A week before Kennedy was shot, where else would he be but with Marilyn Monroe.

Were these incidents pre-ordained, or were they the most amazing coincidences ever recorded? Could some sort of intelligence have been at work above and beyond human understanding within the "Multi Dimensional Universe?"

Many years ago when I was working as a press photographer, furiously shooting pictures and selling my work to magazines and newspapers, I teamed up with another cameraman who approached me after seeing one of my articles in a photographic magazine. We arranged to meet and, after a long discussion, we formed a partnership to cover feature stories, which his wife offered to market. Off we set shooting picture stories left right and centre then developing and printing each evening, and sometimes right through the night in order to get our work into Fleet Street the next day. His wife came back with glowing reports from magazine and newspaper editors regarding our work. Then after a couple of months, I happened to pop into Tit Bits magazine and, on talking to the editor, I asked him when he was going to settle some of our bills for pictures and features used. "Oh," he said, "your colleague called in last week and asked whether we could pay in cash, so I authorized the accounts department to pay up on demand."

On returning to our premises, I casually asked him when Tit Bits would settle our account. His reply was: "Probably in a couple of weeks' time." I knew that he was lying through his back teeth, and I wondered how many more bills had he and his wife intercepted. If I had not personally visited the editor of the magazine, it may have taken me a couple of months to fathom out what was happening to the money. I looked him straight in the eyes and informed him that I had spoken to the editor of Tit Bits, and he said that he had already paid our bills in cash. He went white around the gills and then shot out of my flat like a bullet. He disappeared with hundreds of my pictures and feature stories leaving me to pick up the financial debts.

When I eventually located him, he was living in Broadstairs, which is about eighty miles from London right down in the tip of Kent. I was so mad that I jumped in to my vehicle and high-tailed it towards Broadstairs. On the way down the A2, the cause and effect law started to operate because I developed a flat tyre, was forced change the wheel in a blinding snowstorm, then I was booked for speeding. So when I eventually arrived at the house, I furiously rang the bell. When his wife opened the door, she went white around the gills. "Oh," she gasped. "It's you." I pushed passed her screaming, "Where is he?" She replied, "He is not well and is in bed." I stormed up the stairs and opened one door after another until eventually I found the right bedroom. He was lying on his back with the bedclothes pulled right up to his nose. I reached over and literally ripped off the bedclothes, and there he was, fully dressed with his boots still on his feet. When he heard my irate voice, he must have leapt straight into bed fully

The Multi Dimensional Universe   by   Anthony Malpas   144 clothed in order to obtain a bit of sympathy instead of a thick ear. I demanded the return of my pictures or else, and after retrieving as much material as possible, I departed before I lost my cool altogether. Here was a typical werewolf who had spent his life looking for victims, and I just happened to cross his path at the wrong time. This meant that I had to examine my own personal behaviour in order to avoid future problems.

A year later I wrote a series of articles for The British Journal of Photography pinpointing these events without naming the said werewolf. Soon after out of the blue I received a letter from a photographer, who had read my article, claiming that he recognized the culprit by my description and modus operandi. After comparing notes we realized that we had both been conned by the same werewolf. Another interesting point is that when I first started working as a freelance photographer, I kept on seeing this person's name in dozens of magazines. When he sold a cover picture, I sold a feature story to the same magazine, and when he won a competition, I came second or third; the next time, the order was reversed. So for about five years, we both knew each other's names without ever communicating until my article appeared documenting the above events.

To top it all, how about this for another amazing coincidence

We both had the same birthday of September 20th, we both worked for the same commercial clients, and both sold pictures and feature stories to the same magazines. We both had one son, and they are now both working in the musical world. That was not the last of the said werewolf because when he went to the USA to photograph the Beatles, a baton-swinging cop knocked his camera out of his hand breaking the lever wind so he was only able to obtain a small number of pictures with the reserve camera. Then the editor of the magazine who eventually published his pictures gave himself a by-line instead of the photographer. Later the said werewolf tried a new tack by passing himself off with a false alias when visiting Fleet Street. When my friend visited Fleet Street on a selling expedition and announced his name, every editor said, "You are not JD; he is a short fat man with a bald head and thick glasses." The werewolf was unable to use his own name because of past criminal activities so he passed himself off as another person. Once it was ascertained who was who, the cause and effect law took him out of business because he was always up to every confidence trick imaginable, and helped himself at every opportunity. The Law of Karma never fails; I have seen it working at every level of society.

As you sow, you will reap

My guardian Angel was probably looking after my interests during that encounter because I did not lose too much money, and I was instrumental in publicising his activities.

Car Accidents

My car once caught fire right outside Henley's garage in Kentish Town, so I jumped out, dashed inside the reception area as clouds of smoke erupted from under the bonnet. A mechanic rushed out and immediately disconnected the battery, just in time to save the car, so the only real damage was that I had to get the car rewired.

After that event I decided to consult an astrologer, to ascertain whether he was able to throw any light on my situation. I contacted John Naylor, who was at that time one of Britain's top astrology consultants. I phoned to make an appointment, and eventually turned up at his office adjacent to Harley St, London.

On entering his premises, I was accosted by a very attractive secretary, and observed two typists working flat out in an adjoining office. I was ushered into John's consulting room fully expected to find a yogi-like figure with a flowing beard and white robes floating up near the ceiling. Instead, in front of me, was a beautifully dressed man in a Saville Row suit sitting behind a large modern desk.

He asked me to sit down and ascertained my time, date and place of birth. Then after a few moments of consulting his ephemeris, he pronounced that I was a born writer. I thought he was off his head because I was a photographer, and had never written more than one article in my life. I had no ambitions to be a writer. Then I informed him that my car had recently caught fire and had to be rewired. He stated that it was straws in the wind, and I should take extra care when driving, otherwise I could be involved in an accident on the road.

A few months later, I was driving through Lincoln on my way to Grimsby, and as I approached crossroads with the Cathedral in the distance, I slowed down to check which road to take. The traffic lights were still green, so I proceeded across the junction. Then a vehicle driving in the opposite direction suddenly turned right and swerved across my path. We collided with a bang, smashing my bonnet, front wing and radiator. John Naylor was correct in his assessment of my astrology chart, predicting the possibility of an accident on the road. Now I always check the planetary aspects before any long journey because whenever I have been involved in a car accident or been breathalysed by the police, it has always been when my natal Mars, operating from the third house in my chart and ruling transport and communications, was adversely aspected.

Perhaps I should also have examined my personal behaviour pattern, which could have activated the cause and effect law against me thereby causing the events to happen at the appointed time. Later I took John Naylor's advice regarding the possibility of using photography and journalism as a combined career and, much to my surprise, when I walked into a magazine office with a set of pictures the editor asked me to write an article to go alongside them.

From then on I progressed to writing columns for numerous photographic magazines and even film scripts for the Rank Organisation. Many of my articles were sold on a worldwide basis. To date, this publication will be my eleventh book, so I guess the astrologer was right after all. Then curiosity set me on a path of learning the technicalities of palmistry, astrology and the tarot, which I have used ever since.

Chapter Twenty
The Cause and Effect Law in Politics, plus Government Brainwashing on TV

The system of brainwashing in government is nearly always the same, with a powerful leader continuously bombarding his or her philosophy into the minds of their people until they attach what the ancients called an AKA thread. Thoughts can then be amplified, and through a process of auto-hypnotic suggestion, gain control of people's minds, especially the young and vulnerable. Take a look at the situation in Iraq. When the first Gulf war occurred, and the Iraqi army was destroyed, we did not go straight into Baghdad and eliminate the tyrant in order to set the Iraq people free.

The war was called off before that happened, and the Americans promised to help if the people rose up and deposed the dictator. The Americans later refused to help so Saddam was still able to impose his will with torture and death to all who opposed him.

George Bush only came to power by default. The election was fixed by refusing to allow a vast number of black people to vote, and false information was broadcast over the air suggesting that massive corruption was the reason that Al Gore lost. After George Bush became president, he spent most of his time on holiday, leaving the running of the USA to other people, proving that there was an element of control within the White House outside the President's jurisdiction. After 9/11 when New York was bombed, George Bush had no idea what to do, and constantly relied on his close advisors for any form of action. Also, during the next three days, when all planes in the USA were grounded, only Saudis were allowed to leave the USA without hindrance. Why? Was it because they own around seven percent of the multi-nationals in the USA, which means that after investing their oil money they own billions of American dollars?

The government in power knew this and the Saudis were allowed to leave. Any other nationality connected with the bombing would have been instantly interned.

The Propaganda Machine in Action

A massive propaganda campaign was then waged to instil fear into the American people, diverting the real attention away from the culprits and on to Iraq. The American war machine then went into action without any proof that Iraq was involved in 9/11. To placate the American people, President George Bush decided to invade Iraq, probably to finish the job his father started, to obtain control of the oil industry, to try out the American war machine, and to award massive contracts to government officials for rebuilding the country after the war.

It was quite obvious that it was nothing to do with setting the Iraqi people free because our own Prime Minister Tony Blair would have at his fingertips all possible information regarding the use of nuclear and chemical weapons available to Saddam. The world however watched with amazement on TV as our Prime Minister ignored the advice of his party, the secret service, the majority of his advisors, and the wish of the British people. Pursuing his own personal ambitions he campaigned all over the world in order to gain support from the United Nations to invade Iraq on the basis that the dictator could launch a chemical weapons attack in forty five minutes.

This has subsequently proved to be completely untrue because no weapons of mass destruction were ever found. My question to the Prime Minister is: Why did you not ask to view satellite pictures of Iraq showing whether there were any indications of rocket launching sites, and then present them to the public to justify your claims? If there was no solid evidence of rocket launching sites, then how in hell could the tyrant have launched a rocket in the first place?

To give you an idea of how destructive modern technology can be, and how finely targeted if circumstances suit, just think of what happened to a president of Chechnya. He drove out into the country in order to make a call from his mobile phone, with the idea that it could not be traced. The Russians then located the exact longitude and latitude of the call using satellite transmission, and launched a guided missile programmed to the exact degree of his location. He was eliminated without ever knowing what hit him.

Subsequent problems have now arisen due to the war in Iraq, with British and American servicemen being killed, looting and destruction going on day and night, and with no real success at enforcing law and order. The country has been turned into a complete turmoil making it a target for numerous terrorist groups to operate by uniting in hatred against Western Civilization. Instead of improving the situation, the terrorists are probably planning to retaliate at every opportunity. Also there is now a possibility that a civil war could erupt which just goes to show how blind, arrogant and conceited are the majority of world leaders.

The real problem was that our western leaders had no comprehension that fundamentalists in any religion can so brainwash young people to believe that they will go to heaven if they kill themselves in the service of their faith. Why then do the leaders proposing this philosophy not kill themselves, instead of using simple uneducated souls to do their bidding in the belief that they are doing their religion and country a service? These terrorists are still living in the dark ages, and their philosophy and religion is so divorced from the western world that it may take hundreds of years before the two philosophies link up together, in order to make a better world for the people of planet Earth.

It appears that the USA is not run by their presidents, and any candidate that cannot be manipulated stands no chance of being elected. When President Reagan was in office, he was advised to offer a total guarantee by the USA government, for any loan that the Save and Prosper banks issued to any company in the USA. Can you imagine what happened next? The ministers in government that instigated this guarantee literally approached every available bank, borrowing hundreds of millions, regardless of what the money was to be used for. Then every other wheeler-dealer also flew into the banks, in the knowledge that they did not have to repay any debts. The banks were so obliging because the American government guaranteed to pick up any outstanding debts.

The results of this fiasco were that companies were set up by the thousands, building hotels and towns in the desert that would never make a profit. This unbelievable financial con trick eventually came to light a few years later when the tax authorities started an investigation into why so many massive companies were going bankrupt. When the truth eventually surfaced no one could believe the scale of this scam which left the American government debts of *six hundred billion dollars*. To pay off this massive debt with the final figure probably amounting to over *one trillion dollars* it would take the American public over thirty years of extra taxation just to break even.

The Real Reason for Invading Iraq

How about this for a theory regarding the war in Iraq? After Saddam invaded Kuwait, and was well and truly thrashed, why did we not proceed directly into Baghdad and finish the job of deposing the tyrant? It was illogical to stop half way and let Saddam off the hook to re-arm and start all over again, which could have resulted in a possible invasion of Saudi at a later date.

It was in the American interest to use this possibility to cause fear in that region, so they would have a lever when negotiating deals with the Saudis. Obviously governments never tell the truth regarding what is going on beneath the surface. Suppose a deal was struck between a secret group of American and Saudi billionaires to resurrect the war in Iraq in order to safeguard and control the Middle East's oil production. The American intelligence agencies knew about the possibility of an attack on the mainland by terrorists so why was this not followed up? It was probably all documented and kept under wraps. Why? 9/11 was undoubtedly engineered by a combination of a secret terrorist cell within the USA and an overseas terrorist organization.

The writing was on the wall, with certain government officials turning a blind eye to the events preceding the attack. Afterwards the USA government was looking for a scapegoat to divert attention away from the real terrorists. Also it was in the interests of the Saudis to stop Saddam Hussein from re-arming and invading their country. So to appease the rulers of Saudi, and to justify an invasion of Iraq, the USA went to war without any justification or proof that Saddam Hussein was responsible for 9/11. Also there were no weapons of mass destruction in Iraq. So hundreds, if not thousands of American soldiers, plus thousands of innocent civilians including women and children have been seriously injured or died for nothing.

"Those whom the Gods destroy they first make mad," is very appropriate here. All deeds and words return from whence they came. When I was a child I was very fortunate to be such an awkward and obstinate youngster, and I totally ignored the signals beamed at me by well-meaning adults. This I found out later in life was my salvation for understanding some of the ramifications of the "Multi Dimensional Universe."

The Insidious New British Tax Laws

When any country is vastly over-taxed, and dozens of new laws, rules and regulations are introduced to control the population, there has always been a revolution. Are we in Britain heading in this direction? By the end of 2004, the Institute for Fiscal Studies stated that in Britain, the New Labour Government had introduced at least one hundred-and-fifty-seven new stealth tax laws since it came to power - after promising faithfully not to increase taxes. They have increased national insurance contributions to eight percent of earnings, and changed the basic tax laws, which will crucify many small businesses.

Any person starting up on their own, and then borrowing a great deal of money to keep the business rolling, is being hit with a diabolical tax system at the end of their first financial year. On top of paying income tax for the past year based on profit earned, the government brought in a brand new tax law stating that the equivalent income tax from last year must also be paid in advance of next year's earnings. For instance, one friend earned a net taxable income of around £23,000, and when her tax was assessed, she was forced to pay £5,000, plus another £5,000 in advance of the following year. This situation will eventually result in a vast increase in bankruptcies, or a considerable explosion of the black economy. Tax on wine, spirits, cigarettes, petrol and council tax has risen by seventy percent since New Labour came to power so that with the massive stealth tax increases all round, taxes have risen by approximately £9,000 per annum for the average family. The Chancellor, having plundered government pension funds, is now extorting from the self-employed before it is earned in order to finance his vast overspending. Dick

Turpin is not dead - his followers occupy the majority of seats in the New Fascist Labour Party.

Those whom the Gods destroy they first make mad, and no greater madness has been inflicted on the British public since Margaret Thatcher introduced a new poll tax.
Only recently I read in the national press that a woman had been prosecuted for eating an apple while driving her car, and the police spent ten thousand pounds to prove her guilt. So how long will it take to set in motion the next revolution because, as I have already stated, when the people of any country have been so highly taxed and repressed, a revolution of some sort will always occur.

We in Britain will be no different in the long run. The only problem is why it is taking so long to rouse up British fury at the mind-bending rules and regulations already imposed on us by the un-elected dictators of the EEC. Now they have targeted complementary medicine, and are attempting to stop the sale of certain vitamins and long-standing remedies. That reeks of a conspiracy by the multi-national drug companies to ban the use of many homeopathic cures that have been passed down through the ages. So many of my friends had heart attacks resulting in bypass surgery, and as a result I researched the subject and found that in the 1930's the Shute Foundation in Canada discovered that massive doses of vitamin E would open up the arterial system, dissolve blood clots, lower cholesterol and keep arthritis at bay. This was also researched in Germany, and the same results were found. So preventing a heart attack or eliminating angina costs very little money because Vitamin E capsules can be purchased in any chemist, drug store or supermarket.

When I was twenty-six years of age, I woke up one night with an excruciating pain in my chest. I could hardly breathe and my pulse was very fast and irregular. My wife wanted to call the doctor but I was adamant that it was only indigestion so I lay in bed attempting to relax every muscle in my body and get rid of the problem. Then one afternoon three days later, the doctor appeared and checked my pulse, which by then was still beating very fast but without the irregular pattern. The doctor shipped me off to hospital, and they pumped me full of chemicals. Eventually the pain disappeared, so they sent me home. However, every so often when I was out walking, I received a sudden violent pain in my chest, as though I was hit by a sledge hammer. Then one day I was walking in the local park when I felt a sudden ferocious chest pain which paralyzed me, so that I could hardly breathe. I sat down on a park bench to relax as my arterial system started to close up altogether. Then very slowly I managed to crawl back home, taking about three hours to stagger half a mile. I then had to crawl up four flights of stairs, because my flat was on the top floor. Even though the medics tested me over and over again, this pattern persisted for the next eighteen months. In desperation I decided that I would get myself fit or die in the attempt, so I signed on to play five-a-side soccer, which was about the most lunatic thing possible.

On my first game, I ran around like a madman with sweat dripping out of me by the bucket. On staggering back home I was violently sick, with my pulse racing furiously. Eventually I stretched out in bed wondering whether I would survive through the night. When I woke up next day, I was in a state of great relaxation, and my pulse was beating very slowly and regularly. I wondered whether I was dead or alive. It was only after that incident that I read about the Shute Foundation. I started taking large doses of vitamin E and then my chest pains disappeared altogether. I am still playing football at the age of seventy-four years.

Recently I suffered with a stressful situation, and once again an arterial blockage occurred, with severe chest pains and difficulty breathing. So over a forty-eight hour period, I took five thousand milligrams of vitamin E, and fifteen hundred milligrams of soluble aspirin which totally eliminated the blockage. Later I had an ECG, blood pressure and cholesterol test, and was pronounced perfectly fit with no arterial damage. Why should the Medical Profession not prescribe such a simple remedy? The answer is that the multi-national drug companies promote their drugs without telling the public exactly what type of after-effects could arise. If they told the truth they would lose billions of pounds. Also, most politicians have their pension funds and shares in these companies, so they attempt to discredit and ban any competition which can be obtained at a much lower price.

Modern Day Brainwashing

Have you noticed that New Labour is the largest advertiser on British TV? There is a very good psychological reason for this because every ad you see regarding smoking, cancer and accidents, is designed to instil fear and apprehension into the minds of the public. This in turn will transfer public attention away from the government's hidden agenda. Continuous repetition at prime times will instil considerable fear into many impressionable minds. The Government spend millions telling the public the dangers of smoking tobacco just to prepare for a new law banning smoking in public places, yet they ignore the situation regarding hard drugs that are the real danger to young impressionable people. This shows that they are either out of touch with reality or this is the start of a much greater brainwashing programme. Any person standing on the corner of a road junction will inhale a great deal of carbon monoxide which is a far greater danger than smoking cigarettes. So when will the British government ban the internal combustion engine which causes more pollution and asthma attacks than cigarette smoking?

All over the world there are details of the "Multi Dimensional Universe" filed away in government offices which never come to light because the truth will set the people free. Just look at the Official Secrets Act and realise what it actually means. This Act was made official by parliament in order to protect the royal family, politicians, and members of the elite ruling classes from public exposure. Now the official secrets act has been changed giving the public access to official records. However, any government can still withhold certain information if it thinks that they could be embarrassed by exposure to the press and public. Certain countries can and do torture and kill human beings in order to make them confess to crimes they did not commit. Yet as long as those countries buy weapons of war and business products, the politicians in the western world throw all morality out of the window, and are in reality just as guilty of torture and murder as the perpetrators. Because they do nothing! For instance, people who voted the new labour party back into power in 2004 little realised that all the promises made in order to gain power have now been broken over and over again. Every day brings more atrocities for both soldiers and civilians in Iraq; killed by brainwashed psychopathic killers. In Britain, crime figures and hard drug pushing are rising, criminals are given minute sentences, and their anti-social activities are looked on liberally. Innocent people have little or no protection against burglars or robbers who are given license to take legal action, if in the course of their crimes they get injured by their victims.

I was recently talking to a London police detective who stated that, in his opinion, the law was absolutely loaded in favour of the criminal. For instance, when Holly and Jessica were killed by their school caretaker, Ian Huntley, the police in one county were not allowed to pass on any suspicions regarding the possibility that this man was dangerous. There was a law stating that information cannot be passed down the line unless a conviction has occurred, and it was this law in operation that was responsible for the course of events that led to the murder of two innocent young girls. Also, I was informed that if a British detective wanted to check on the possibility of criminal activity by any known criminal operating in Britain and the USA, the FBI, CIA or any other police force in the USA will instantly pass on any information they have in their files regarding the said person whether they have or have not been convicted.

Yet if any other overseas police force or government agency asks for information from Britain, our police do not have the authority to pass on any suspicions, which means that unless a criminal has a police record of convictions British police are completely handicapped in their efforts to prevent certain types of criminals committing murder in the future. How can any government allow such a terrible law to remain on the statute books for so long? I was also informed that if a criminal is caught in the act of committing a serious crime on camera, the judge could rule that the images are inadmissible if the camera is in a public place. So that even if the police have absolute concrete evidence against a known criminal, a very smart lawyer can have the evidence suppressed so that the jury will have no knowledge that the criminal was actually filmed in the act. All through history you will find that when the people are oppressed and taxed to hell, a revolution occurs. How long will it take for the government in power to get the message that even they too are governed by the cause and effect law, and their resulting actions will eventually rebound back upon them?

The interesting thing here is that, until recently, the present Labour government had no opposition voicing its wrath at the way the country was being run. On that evidence one would assume that the leaders of the opposition, and the Prime Minister, belonged to the same club or secret society, and did not want to rock the boat.

The Poll Tax Disaster
Look what happened when Mrs Thatcher was Prime Minister of Britain. She decided to eliminate council tax, changed the rules and introduced a poll tax. So instead of property owners paying a set council tax, every member of the household had to pay a separate tax. This meant that if four people lived in one property, each person would be individually liable for extra tax. I wondered whether she ever read history because in the Middle Ages when a poll tax was introduced in Britain a bloody revolution took place. Her general life was so different and isolated from the people of Britain that she was totally unable to ascertain the probable outcome of this taxation system. How could a multi-millionaire family understand the problems of the unemployed or low paid workers? In ethnic communities like Brixton, with many people living in the same house, how on earth did she expect the government to collect those taxes? All over Britain, thousands of people just refused to pay, and to send in the bailiffs would have resulted in riots, bloodletting, and a possible civil war. Eventually the law of cause and effect started working, and this act of parliament was her political downfall.

"Those whom the Gods destroy they first make mad."
So ended Mrs Thatcher's political career as Prime Minister. Also, during the Thatcher government, council houses were put up for sale so that tenants could take out a mortgage and become house owners. This sparked off a massive round of buying and selling which in turn set in motion inflation on a grand scale. Today in 2006, few young couples can afford to buy their own house or flat especially in London unless they are earning around one hundred thousand pounds or more per annum, and even then they would be hard pushed to pay the mortgage. Also a vast amount of council property has been allocated to asylum seekers, young pregnant teenagers, ethnic minorities, and the disabled. In fact I know of one person suffering with arthritis that not only lives in a council house, but is also given a new car provided

by the taxpayer with the blessing of the government. Probably the greatest confidence trick played by governments is in doctoring all the numbers of asylum seekers. Unemployment figures are also doctored to let the government move numbers sideways, taking out many areas of the population and thereby giving a false impression of the true facts. Potential growth figures are also exaggerated which is why there are so many problems for people who took out insurance mortgages, leaving thousands of people ending up with negative equity when their policy is paid up. Then the biggest con of all is the inflation figures because they do not include the cost of property so that successive governments, most of which have investments in property corporations and individual houses, are delighted that their ever-increasing investments are hidden from the public. If the truth came out, the unions would scream blue murder and demand massive wage increases to cover the real inflation figures.

I read in the Daily Express that seven hundred speed cameras had been destroyed, not by young vandals but by honest hard working people who felt so repressed, they stood up and decided to retaliate. This is only the start of the revolution, which we can only hope does not accelerate violently in the near future. The law of Karma has already started to evolve, and will multiply to such a degree, that the ruling classes have no idea of what will eventually hit them. Any government that keeps increasing taxes to pay for their personal financial failure will cause great anger and ferocity at each unjust action.

The British people pay a vast amount of hidden taxes, and then when they die, their children are faced with an inheritance tax. I wonder why these blind politicians cannot see the wood for the trees regarding this situation. The war in Iraq was nothing to do with weapons of mass destruction, or to free the people from a vicious tyrant. What did the western world do when China invaded Tibet? Absolutely nothing because China was a massive business market for western governments, so no word of condemnation was spoken. Look at the terrible wars and suffering in Africa where dictators torture and kill millions of innocent people, yet western governments do exactly nothing until it is too late. If there is no oil under the ground, there is no point invading any country. Control of the oil, use of the latest weapons, and money made by the giant construction companies when the war was over was the real reason for the war in Iraq, and the blind politicians were so arrogant that did not take into consideration the will of the people.

President Bush and Tony Blair have now created a massive gulf between the West and Muslim countries with terrible consequences from terrorist activities in the future. A new Vietnam or Korea, which could lead up to a third world war, may well be present in the not too distant future. We have also heard that certain offices in the United Nations were bugged prior to the war. I am not in the least surprised at this revelation because almost every person in government and every office would automatically be bugged. Also every landline telephone in Britain will have some kind of bugging device in the exchange, so that the central computer will pick up certain words, which could be interpreted as a possible threat to security. We can expect that, sometime in the future, every phone call will be recorded and analysed.

George Orwell was not wrong in his assessment of the future except that he got his dates wrong. It was not 1984, but many years later that the seeds for total control of the population is being implemented, with possible ID cards, micro chips, and tags being introduced so that honest people have no chance of evading this massive government control. Also, we are brainwashed into believing that we must have a university education. Why? Not every person is suitable for higher education, and the apprentice schemes of long ago have fallen by the wayside. When non-academic people are brainwashed into attending a university they are told that without a degree they will never progress financially. This is absolute rubbish because in my profession of photography, when students graduate with a degree in photography and fine art, only fifteen percent are able to find a job in professional photography. The other eighty-five percent end up working in camera shops as sales assistants, or other similar jobs.

What motive could any government have in persuading the majority of people that they need a university education?
The answer is very simple because, when a student graduates, he or she will have racked up massive debts, which have at some time in

the future to be paid. This means that a student must get a job, which also means that they are paying Income Tax, VAT and National Insurance Tax. Then they are persuaded to take out a mortgage so that their income is sealed for many years, with successive governments taking a massive slice of future income from direct and indirect taxes. This great confidence trick means that governments can make a guess at the state of the economy based on false figures for the future. They brainwash people into taking out long-term bank and credit card loans without which the British government would collapse overnight because they would collect far less taxes. That would mean extra government borrowing to top up the economy, or the unthinkable could happen. The government would have to cut its overheads, and account for all its expenditure in order to make ends meet.

During the past few years, the British government, and many large companies have siphoned off billions of pounds from government and public company pension funds, leaving such a shortfall, that no pensions are safe.

Many of my friends who paid into an insurance or company pension fund on the promise that they would receive a specific amount per annum on retirement have been deeply shocked. In many cases only half or less has been paid to them when the policy matures than promised. This is selling on false pretences and would be liable for prosecution in any other business. Now we are bombarded by government advertisements telling young people to pay a larger percentage of their income into a pension fund in order to avoid poverty in their old age. Why now, after all the skulduggery in the pensions industry has come into the open? The answer is very simple: the government needs the extra increase in pensions, not to help people in the future when they retire, but to pay for the present shortfall of funds now. So this means that unless the system is changed, people paying into pension funds now will need a future generation to pay even more money into pension funds to cover their pensions when they are due.

Look at the inoculation fiasco. Why should the British Labour government demand that a parent subject their child to the three-in-one vaccination? Also, why are professors of science and medicine seen on TV, stating that there is no evidence of any problems with this system? Then the Prime Minister and Chancellor refused to answer the press whether their children had been given the three-in-one jab. By refusing to answer the direct question, it was quite apparent that they had both opted for three separate injections. There have been so many discussions regarding the three-in-one jab by so many educated people on TV arguing for its validity but, with one accord, I have never heard an academic, scientist or politician, state the obvious.

Can the immunization system of a baby take three different viruses at the same time, without any adverse effects?
So why not give the baby one injection, enabling its system to cope, before the second, then the third, because all three at one time could put too much strain on the child's immunisation system? Why take the risk? The answer is obviously that it costs the government more money to administer three separate injections than the three-in-one. Also, if a vast stock of the serum had already been manufactured at government expense, the safety of the child will be of secondary importance.

Again, the manufacturing drug companies run the National Health Service with incentives for medical professionals and politicians. They call it lobbying but in reality it is bribery on a grand scale. Many politicians will have massive investments in the drug industry so it is in their financial interests to foster the three-in-one recommendation as standard and safe. The New Labour Government is attempting to take away the right of parents to choose the correct system for their child, so once again we have more government interference. When are they going to learn that they can brainwash most of the people most of the time, but they cannot brainwash all the people all of the time?

As I am checking this chapter for the last time, results of the British local elections in May 2006 were announced. When I went to the polling station to register my vote, many people who were staunch labour supporters stated that they would never vote for the party ever again because the lies, deception and controls that the party had implemented during the past nine years. Sure enough the cause and effect law kicked in, with Labour taking a terrible beating losing many of the councils that they had controlled for over thirty years. Tony Blair then informed the press that he was shuffling his cabinet, in an attempt to gain control before the next general election, and one wit stated that it was like shuffling deck chairs on the Titanic before it sank. The journal Private Eye recently published a cartoon that depicted the labour lunatics very accurately. A government official was seen interviewing a householder claiming that it was illegal not to have a ramp installed into his house specially for disabled burglars in wheelchairs. This accurately depicts the level of government pandering to the criminal elements in our society.

Hitler set the Second World War in motion because Germany was subjected to considerable oppression by the French and British governments and the international bankers during the 1920's. Due to the terrible restrictions imposed by the allies, the rate of inflation was so high that a Swiss student was able to buy a row of houses with his educational grant, which meant that the German people were starving. Then the cause and effect law started to operate, as numerous political parties fought for power, and out of the destruction and desolation rose the Nazi party led by the fanatical Hitler.

The Nazi party would never have come to power in the first place, if the allies had treated Germany with honesty and respect after the First World War. The allies made no effort to help Germany back to a reasonable level of financial independence. So the law of cause and effect started operating in very quick time, and we all know the results. The total stupidity, arrogance and blindness of the British and French governments during that period created the perfect situation for a revolution, and that is exactly what occurred with devastating consequences.

Government Deception During the First World War.
During the First World War, T.E. Lawrence, known as Lawrence of Arabia, led an army of Arabs against the Turks in order to help the British war effort. The British and French promised that the Arabs would have a government of their own after the war was over, and so on this promise they followed Lawrence into battle. When victory was eventually won, the British and French governments broke their

promises, and took control of the Middle East, so the cause and effect law was once again set in motion with devastating future consequences.

Both the French and Russian revolutions were caused by the conceit and arrogance of the ruling classes who applied vicious controls and taxes. Eventually the people rose up and slaughtered a generation of those stupid blind greedy rulers. Nothing is ever what it seems on the surface because the present British economy is based on enslaving the population by devious means, such as offering massive loans through mortgages, banks and credit cards, so that people are well and truly trapped by the system, racking up massive debts in order to keep the government supplied with Tax! Tax! Tax! to squander at will.

If the real figure is worked out exactly, then how much money the government steals would amount to around twenty-five thousand pounds or more per head of the population, per annum. That is reaped, as previously stated, from Income Tax, National Insurance, VAT and Duty, as they call it, on vehicles; TV licences, tax on computers, petrol, alcohol, tobacco and thousands of other products. Then there are other licenses for various items, speeding fines and parking fines. Plus there is a mortgage or rent, and council tax. So, as well as removing around twenty-five thousand pounds from your pocket, on a sixty-thousand pound income, the government still borrow billions of pounds from the international monetary fund, in order to finance its massive overspending and miscalculation on future growth. Then the public will pay interest on those loans in the form of increased taxes. This is caused by a conspiracy between the banks, the multi-national companies and governments. When a bank loans out money to the public in the form of credit cards at an exhorbitant rate of interest, they are not really borrowing hard cash, just statements on a piece of paper because the actual money does not exist. It gives people a false sense of security, that they can purchase a new car, an expensive holiday, a new house, new furniture, and climb on board the ever-increasing gravy train, with the blessing of successive governments.

Without the massive expansion of manufactured goods, and collecting tax on a vast scale, the government would go bankrupt overnight.

Obviously this situation cannot go on forever, and when the crash occurs the government will have to increase taxes even further, to pay for their vast overspending. It is not whether it will happen, the question is when?

The year 2007 to 2008 may be the period that could bring the present Labour Government to its knees, mainly due to its miscalculation of future growth figures. It will be interesting to see whether the British stock market will falter between December 2006 and the spring of 2007 because there is a possibility that the planetary aspects are adverse for the City of London.

Whilst I was checking this chapter before sending the manuscript to the publisher, the government announced that a complete ban on cigarette smoking in public places would soon be in place. After spending millions of pounds conducting a brainwashing campaign on TV, pinpointing the dangers of smoking, they totally ignored the dangers of the internal combustion engine. Parents pushing a pram along the pavement with vehicles passing nearby will cause their child much more harm than any cigarette smoke. Also, the harm if you stand on the corner of Trafalgar Square, with thousands of buses, taxis and lorries belching out diesel and petrol fumes - the government has totally ignored this very dangerous situation.

When they checked pollution from toxic exhaust fumes, they placed numerous meters high up on buildings, well above the roadway, then pronounced there was no real danger. When the RAC and the AA checked the volume of pollution, they placed their meters at ground level and found that the pollution increased to a very dangerous level. So when will the British Government ban the internal combustion engine?

Local Governments

Local governments are notorious for wasting taxpayers' money. Just look at a few examples. For instance, millions of pounds have been have been spent all over Britain placing bumps on side roads in the mistaken belief that they are saving lives by slowing down traffic, whilst at the same time leaving potholes in between the bumps for unsuspecting motorists, causing damage to tyres and suspension.

They do not take into consideration that the majority of accidents occur at road junctions by reckless driving and tailgating, especially in bad weather. It is not just speed that is dangerous; it is the illogical thinking of those in power that causes most damage.

Just ask any ambulance driver or paramedic rushing to an accident or attempting to take a badly injured or seriously ill person to hospital. It has been estimated that the speed bumps have resulted in at least five hundred deaths; also what about fire engines? If your property is on fire, the speed bumps slow the fire engines down, and so by the time they arrive your house could be well and truly on fire. Again if you are burgled, the police will take longer to get to their destination because they too have to navigate the speed bumps. At night especially in wet conditions, when vehicles are approaching on the opposite side of the road, they ride up over the bumps, and their headlights also rise and dazzle drivers coming in the opposite direction creating a further dangerous situation. What about the noise and damage to vehicles as they bounce over the bumps, especially vehicles with a low sump and exhaust systems? Also what about the increased noise created by heavy lorries bouncing and crashing over the bumps? What about bus passengers who have to stand the bouncing upheaval every time the vehicle climbs over a bump, and the injuries caused by this movement.

One friend was badly injured when a bus bounced over a series of bumps, she fell injuring her ribs and was in severe pain for months afterwards. Sooner or later local councils will be inundated with legal action from injured parties caused by these road bumps. Every time an ambulance arrives late resulting in a person dying, the legal implications will eventually cost millions. Who do you think will foot that series of legal actions and settlements? Also when a vehicle reaches a speed bump, it often slows up, and then accelerates furiously right up to the next bump, creating a vast obnoxious emission of extra pollution due to the increased revving of the engine. These points were never discussed when the idea for millions of road bumps was commissioned. What a money-spinner for friends and relatives of local councils, working in the construction business.

Probably hundreds of millions of pounds have been wasted over the last twenty years, which could have been put to more useful projects. Unfortunately the road surfaces are often so neglected that vehicles have not only to navigate the ups and downs of the bumps, but also have to negotiate the dangerous hazard of huge potholes in between. Years ago I had a friend working for a Manchester corporation, where he handled all their publicity, so he set up his own business as a supplier and handed out contracts to himself. This you will find goes on at every level of business, government departments, and local councils are no exception.

The London Congestion Charge

Look what happened when Mayor Livingstone brought in London traffic congestion charges. To justify his cause, he changed the timing of traffic lights, causing extra congestion throughout the city, thereby attempting to justify his actions. However, it has produced far less tax than was first estimated, and a drop in revenue for many local businesses. Then the charges were increased from five to eight pounds, and he is now attempting to extend the area even further and increase the charge to ten pounds or even twenty-five pounds, together with the number the number of parking meters and parking charges.

The cause and effect law will at some time start operating, possibly with disastrous effects for Mayor Livingstone, either in his capacity as Mayor or his health will deteriorate. Over one thousand black cab taxi drivers received fines for driving in bus lanes, so they stopped the traffic in central London, and their union went to law to defend the rights of every driver. One taxi driver showed me a massive file of papers going backwards and forwards to and from his union, the council, solicitors and a separate adjudicator. Finally his appeal was recognised, and he was exonerated. We are talking about a cost of probably ten thousand pounds per fine. Mayor Livingstone has once again triggered the cause and effect law against himself, which could be another nail in his political coffin.

Recently, I heard on the radio that Barnet council are going to get rid of their speed bumps, but Camden are planning to increase theirs. For many years Brent in North London had been a safe labour seat in Parliament yet, due to Tony Blair's unpopularity regarding the war in

Iraq, in 2004 the Liberals won with a considerable majority, and the Conservative party came a long way back in third place. This was due to a complete lack of leadership, first by William Hague, and then by Ian Duncan Smith, who called himself the quiet man. He was so quiet, you hardly knew he existed. So the law of cause and effect rose up and removed him from office. At the end of 2004 Michael Howard became the new conservative leader and started to give the Labour government a bit of opposition. However, he also has left the opposition leadership, and David Cameron has been elected leader.

Both local and national governments are taking a leaf out of the EEC, by increasing the size of their staff to a massive level, so it means that each new member of staff will be paid a first-class salary, long holidays, vast expenses, and eventually will pick up a large pension. So what will this massive increase in bureaucracy mean? The answer of course is that new laws, rules and regulations will continue to increase, as this lunacy gathers momentum, and common sense is thrown out of the window.

The Ethnic Problem

Another interesting series of events occurred when an ethnic family comprising husband, and wife and two children, one of which was disabled, moved into a block of flats in North London. From that moment all hell was let loose because the wife started burning wood on her electric stove, which resulted in smoke pouring out of her kitchen window, filtering through upstairs bedroom windows in the middle of the night. Other residents woke up coughing and spluttering, wondering where the fumes were coming from. The fire brigade was called out, and the woman was asked to refrain from burning wood on her stove. This warning had no effect, and when her neighbour in the flat directly below complained, she was kicked in the stomach and suffered continuous verbal abuse. Again the fire brigade was called out, but the local council, police, and social services totally ignored the possibility that this woman could start a major fire, and burn the block down.

They were an ethnic family, and had a disabled child, so in the eyes of the so-called politically correct liberal left; they could do no wrong. The wife then started to complain that her flat was broken into, and her furniture and clothes had been cut up. From a psychological point of view it was obvious that this was a disturbed mind, continuously talking about people cutting up her furniture and clothes. Could she be thinking of retaliation because the neighbours dared to call out the fire brigade? The cause and effect law often gives an indication of future events by the shadows cast before the deed is done. Who or what was this very disturbed woman planning to cut up? Next, the long-term tenants in the block kept pots of plants on the window sills. Suddenly they all disappeared, and were found smashed to pieces on the ground floor. Everyone knew who was responsible, but social services and the local council did nothing. By now the police, social services, the fire brigade, and the local council, all had a large file of information regarding this person's behaviour but still nothing was done. Then for the third time, she set fire to her stove, and with smoke pouring out of her kitchen, and the fire brigade was once again called out. The inside of her flat was filled with junk, and was in a terrible state. Her husband was unkempt with long scruffy hair, and was often heard screaming as she attacked him. When the third fire was extinguished, a fireman left and was heard to say. "Now I have seen the real Munsters." The plants on the window sills were eventually replaced, only to be hurled out into the roadway, and once again smashed to bits. Visitors to the block of flats were verbally and physically abused, then a tenant's car was vandalized, causing about £600 worth of damage.

One tenant accosted the said lady on the fire escape, and politely asked whether she had seen the missing plants. She stated that a short dark Jew climbed up the fire escape. She said that she knew he was a Jew because he had a large nose, and he then threatened herself and her children with a gun before stealing the plants. This statement was relayed to the authorities, who once again totally ignored the situation. Then just before Christmas, all the telephones lines in the block went dead, and when the engineers were called out, they found that the wires had been deliberately cut in four different places just outside the problem woman's kitchen, underneath the windows in her first floor lounge, outside her bedroom windows, and outside her bathroom windows, which would have needed a fireman's ladder to scale from the outside. So they could only have been severed from inside her flat!

By now the local council, social services, the police and the fire brigade were inundated with complaints. Then council and social workers started to interview people in the block. Their official attitude to people who complained was so vindictive that they sounded like prosecuting lawyers. Did you see her cutting the telephone lines? Did you see her throwing plants into the road? Did you see her causing damage to the neighbour's car? Many witnesses saw her attacking a neighbour, and heard her verbal abuse, but the government officials were not in the least interested in truth or fair play, only the vindication of this very disturbed ethnic woman, with a disabled child. The police were in reality powerless to interfere because of legal implications, whilst the council and social workers stuck their heads in the sand and refused to do anything.

However, the problem was resolved when a letter stating full details of the previous events written by a psychologist was sent to the chief executive of the council asking who was responsible for seeing that the said woman received and took her medication? Because after the mass of evidence provided, if any child or person was harmed, or the block was set on fire, the council and social services would be liable for massive damages. Obviously the seriousness of the situation regarding possible legal action against the council and social services came home to the chief executive, and then suddenly the family departed. They were never seen again. They were relocated to another area. What sort of society do we have when honest people causing no trouble to any one are subjected to such abuse? Look carefully at the antics of national and local governments and see if you can spot the problems that they may create for themselves in the future. When any organisation misuses its power, the Law of Karma is set in motion. Countries and governments rise and fall because ruthless people who seem to thrive at first always fall in the end.

If a government deals with people fairly, without increasing taxes, and applying rules and regulations in order to benefit the people they serve, they will always stay in power longer than those with a ruthless, dominating and controlling streak. The Law of Karma never fails.

Chapter Twenty-One
Astro Analysis of The EEC

The EEC came into being as a result of the Treaty of Rome signed by six nations, on 25th March 1957 at 18.30 hrs. Saturn the great planet of fate was situated at 14 degrees Sagittarius, less than four degrees from an opposition of the degree ruling the city of London, which is 17 degrees 54 minutes of Gemini. That moment in time had great significance for the British people because it will eventually cause great business losses in the City of London. Then later it was transferred to Brussels, and came into existence in its present form on January 1st 1958 at 00.00 hrs. On January 22nd 1972, Britain signed the Treaty of Brussels, joining the common Market from January 1st 1973 when Saturn was situated at 15 degrees Gemini. This was just two degrees from a conjunction of the degree ruling the City of London. Saturn is the great planet of fate, and any business venture started with an adverse Saturn, usually ends in tears.

On June 6th 1975 twenty-ix million people voted in a referendum for continued membership of the Common Market. In the referendum, 62.2 percent voted in favour and 32.8 percent against. We were not told the truth, or the real intentions of the EEC, so those decisions, plus transferring our currency into decimalisation, caused a vast increase in the cost of almost every commodity, and the British pound was devalued by almost fifty percent!

The Prime Minister was Edward Heath, and he stated that changing to decimalisation would not affect the pound in our pockets. This was either a deliberate lie, or a total miscalculation on the part of the Prime Minister.

An astrological analysis from the date the treaty of Rome was signed may throw some light on the activities and future of the EEC.

Sun............4 degrees 50 minutes   Aries
Moon.........3 degrees 4 minutes   Aquarius
Mercury......9 degrees 58 minutes   Aries
Venus........29 degrees 47 minutes   Pisces

Mars..........4 degrees 56 minutes   Gemini
Jupiter.......25 degrees 50 minutes Virgo   Retro
Saturn.......14 degrees 18 minutes   Sagittarius Retro
Uranus........2 degrees 57 minutes   Leo   Retro
Neptune......1 degree 55 minutes   Scorpio   Retro
Pluto.........28 degrees 22 minutes Leo   Retro

North Node of Moon...22 degrees 16 minutes   Scorpio

South Node of Moon ...22 degrees 16 minutes Taurus

Ascendant   17 degrees 57 minutes Libra
Midheaven   21 degrees 12 minutes Cancer

Element designations:

Fire   5
Earth   1
Air   2
Water   2

Cardinal   2
Fixed   4
Mutable   4

Major Planetary Aspects

The Sun was in 4th degree of Aries which is a fire sign, in a wide conjunction with Mercury at 9 degrees Aries, plus Venus at 29 degrees Pisces. This group of three planets is in brilliant aspect to both the Moon in the 3rd degree of Aquarius, which is an air sign, and Uranus in the 2nd degree of Leo, another fire sign plus an aspect to Mars in the 4th degree of Gemini.

So the fiery, all-out action nature of the EEC promotes a ferocious expansion and an ever increasing revenue. This is magnified by Mercury, the planet of commerce and communication, which is also in brilliant aspect to the business planet Saturn, creating a massive long-term expansion of commerce within the community.

The Elements
There are five planets in Fire signs, and only one in Earth which is the stabilising element, so there is great emphasis on action, movement and expansion, with less emphasis on practical management and financial control. Without a grounding of the Earth element the enthusiasm generated by an unbalanced number of fire elements will run away like an out of control forest fire.

A Jump in First Organization
Without this overwhelming focus on the brilliant aspects of six planets I doubt whether the EEC could have survived because it is essentially a jump-in-head-first organization, which is exactly what the fire elements promote, with Aries, the all-action fire sign of the zodiac most prominent.

Analysis of the Remaining Planets
Having firstly looked at the brilliant expansive aspects we must now analyse the remaining planetary configurations to find out where the EEC is going, and whether the expansion will continue.

Saturn, the planet of restriction, is not called the great teacher for nothing, and is situated in the second house of finance. This is not a good position for long-term money, but it is in excellent aspect to Mercury, the planet of commerce. Even though both planets are fire signs, Saturn rules Capricorn and Mercury rules Virgo, and both are earth signs, so this will promote an expansion of finance connected with property and agriculture. Saturn is also in great aspect to the EEC's ascendant in Libra. This is the benevolent face that the EEC presents to the public with promises of expansion and wealth for all.

Scorpio is on the cusp of the EEC's second house of finance, and its ruler Pluto throws a great aspect to Neptune in Scorpio, so once again we have a continuing increase in revenue with a vast amount of new ingenious methods of raising money. Also, Jupiter the great planet of expansion, is in excellent aspect to the Moon creating a vast amount of public relations and publicity aimed at the housewives of Europe, to persuade people to vote for an ever-expanding EEC. So far the picture looks like a huge financial success. However, now we come to the adverse aspects in order to find out the other side of the coin.

The Adverse Aspects

Firstly, Pluto is adverse to Mars from the eleventh house of friends to the eighth house of long-term investments. The eighth house also includes the south node of the Moon, which is the place where financial resources, and long-term investments disappear down a black hole. This is not a good sign for any long-term investments.

A Dangerous T Square Aspect

One very difficult aspect for any business to overcome is a T square. The EEC has the Moon in the fourth house, ruling the public, women, liquids and property, in opposition to Uranus in the tenth house, ruling the career and long-term business of the EEC. Then Neptune the planet of illusion is square to this opposition, and rules the ocean, fishing, and the drug industry. The adverse square, and the aspects to both Moon and Uranus, promote a vast business illusion followed ultimately by a massive final crash.

Jupiter Aspects

Jupiter, the great planet of luck and abundance, is in opposition to Venus, ruling the Libra ascendant. Venus also influences the Taurus-ruled cusp of the eighth house of long-term investment. What a roller coaster of a ride!

This basic analysis suggests that the EEC will continue expanding regardless of any consequences. However, the great illusion fostered on the public that it is financially beneficial to become a fully fledged member of the EEC is very misleading. This illusion will eventually be shattered because Uranus always brings sudden shocks to any business or person. Some shocks will end up very beneficial, and others will end up in ruin. When the illusions of the EEC are eventually brought out into the open, and a full accounting is demanded by member states, the outcome will shatter the illusions of the politicians and the public. I believe personally that the object of the EEC is to create a United States of Europe with total legal and financial control from Brussels which will destroy the sovereignty of all the countries involved. When this comes out it will indeed shock.

The Original Idea of the EEC

The idea of a group of countries establishing a trading block enabling each nation to trade freely without restrictions is a brilliant idea. However, the truth is rather different because the European Economic Community as it stands today is nothing short of a thief's paradise where confidence tricksters can milk the community dry, with the blessing of the Brussels Bureaucrats.

Never in the history of the human race have the people of Europe been sold down the river by the politicians and bureaucrats with such arrogance.

The cost of food products controlled by the European Cartel could easily be halved in price without this top-heavy lunatic bureaucracy dictating terms to appease the French and German land-owning farming community, which keeps them in power.

The True Facts of Decimalisation
Before Britain decimalised our currency, I could purchase eight pounds of fish for my cat for a one-pound note. Within three months, I could only purchase just over four pounds in weight for one pound of money. This principle was extended to thousands of products within a few months, so it was also a charter for the multi-national companies to increase prices, and decrease the weight in food packages right across the board. The politicians deliberately told the British public that decimalisation would not affect the pound in our pockets. This has now been proved to be a pack of lies, just to get the British public to vote for inclusion into membership of the EEC.

Confidence Tricks
When I was on Jury service, one man informed me that his job was driving a large truck from England to Scotland and back many times each week. When large freezer warehouses in London storing meat carcasses were full, they were emptied, and their products dumped outside to defrost. His job was to transport the carcasses to Scotland, where they were burnt, so that a production line of meat could be continuously stored, then destroyed in order to keep prices artificially high. For years, breeding cattle had been shipped from Ireland to the Continent, and for every shipment the owners received a subsidy from Brussels. When a new vet was appointed to check the cattle, he found that they were gelded. For years, false statements had been made

keeping this financial roller coaster in place, and we paid the price. As one Irish farmer stated with a smile on his face, "We send the cattle in one truck, and the balls in another."

Where are our famous apple orchards? It does not suit the French for us to grow and sell our own apples because their products can be imported to Britain at a much higher price, so Brussels organised the destruction of our much-loved apple orchards. Our home-grown strawberries they said should be heart shaped, and not too square, and then they demanded that cucumbers should be straightened out and not too bent.

Businesses are closed down if the Brussels regulations are not implemented, so our British way of life is being slowly eroded. We are now informed that market traders are not allowed to sell food in pounds and ounces. Our beef was banned by the European Dictators while allowing their own products safe harbour, despite the continued outbreaks of diseased cattle in their countries caused by the continued unnatural feeding of offal and added hormones to herbivores in order to increase weight for extra profit. Interfering with the natural feeding habits of cattle will result in future problems which are now surfacing. Butter mountains were built up and sold off to Russia in order to keep the price artificially high.

Wine lakes were poured down the drain, rather than sell at a commercially fair price. Our fishing industry has almost been destroyed by the Brussels bureaucrats by allowing foreign trawlers to poach our territorial waters.

Recently I read in the Sunday Mail that the ministers in Brussels want to stop the sale of vitamins in British health shops. *Have you ever heard of such madness?* When are the British Politicians going to tell the Fascist Continental Commissars to get lost because the majority of British people want to govern themselves? Is there a political party that pledges itself to reverse all the stupid EEC rules that we have bombarded us: take Britain out of the EEC, close the frontiers to further immigration, and promise to publish full details of the Official Secrets Act? Demand a full investigation into the real inflation figures, (including the true house inflation figures)? Stop the banks and insurance companies from thieving the public with their financial tricks, such as paying investors a pittance of interest, whilst at the same time charging the public a massive uncontrolled high interest; enabling banks and insurance companies to make billions.

This is not a socialist country anymore; it is fast becoming a fascist state, ruled by the New Fascist Labour Government, and the faceless un-elected EEC dictators.

This seems to be the opinion of almost every person I speak to in London. Voices of discontent are getting louder by the day because the politicians in power totally ignore the will of the people.

Not long ago an accountant was given the task of investigating the finances of the EEC, and found so many discrepancies in their accounting system that you could drive a Jumbo jet through the holes. Before any adjustments could be made in order to keep track of the billions of pounds that had gone missing, the good lady accountant was sacked. Why?

My father fought in the last world war to avoid continental dictatorship coming to Britain. Our politicians have up to now meekly submitted to the new EEC fascist dictators living off the greatest gravy train in history at the expense of all the people of Britain and Europe.

For the sake of humanity, call a halt to this lunacy and get the hell off this unbelievable path leading to national bankruptcy.

No greater indication of financial insanity has ever been seen on this planet than the EEC Common Agricultural Policy.

The common agricultural policy was originally organised to benefit French farmers and land owners who collect a vast subsidy in order to keep their own personal gravy train on the rails, at the expense of the public. Wake up you British politicians before it is too late because the revolution is surely on its way! No public liability company could survive with a turnover of over sixty five billion pounds, and allow their directors to milk the company without keeping an accurate accounting of where the money was going. Yet the unelected EEC Bureaucrats do not allow outside accountants to analyse their spending. So they are financially accountable to no one.

Will the EEC survive and prosper as an organisation, or will the bureaucrats take complete control? Will they succeed in unifying all the countries implicated into a United States of Europe with total financial and legal control over all the member countries?

The astrological signs say that the EEC can only survive in the long term if there is a strict accounting system to stop the continued waste of money which usually ends up in the large salaries of beaurocrats, with vast expenses and massive pensions. Grants are also given to the many countries that support the unaccounted continuous spending which amounts to billions of pounds every year. Only when the financial dictators are brought to book, and every penny accounted for, will the people of the EEC start to prosper, otherwise the organisation will end up totally bankrupt including all the member countries.

In January 2005 the EEC was still on a roller coaster, with a major trine aspect between progressed Jupiter and the progressed Sun. This is followed by other beneficial progressed aspects up to the year 2008. However, in between these major beneficial aspects there will be a few problems because in 2005 Saturn joins the midheaven of the EEC chart, then in July and August, operating from the tenth house, it triggers the adverse T square aspect, when it conjuncts the EEC's natal Uranus, opposes its Moon and squares up its Neptune. Problems will then start to appear at the very heart of the EEC, affecting the health of the organisation; which will change the public's perception.

During November and December 2005, Jupiter joins the EEC's Natal Neptune, also affecting the T square adverse aspect increasing problems within the organisation In 2006 and 2007, Pluto in Sagittarius triggers the EEC's Jupiter-Venus opposition affecting the twelfth and sixth houses. This area covers the secrets and health of the EEC, and during that period there may be some indication of corruption revealed. So eventually a team of accountants will descend on the EEC demanding access to their accounts. The dictators of the EEC will do everything in their power to resist this intrusion, but to no avail because at some time in the future, the EEC will have to account for its vast restrictive practices and over expenditure in all directions. The cartels within the organisation will be brought out into the open, so that the public can see for themselves exactly how the money has been managed.

So between 2008 and 2010, there will be a vast accounting, and a possible massive crash or change of direction. Then Britain will probably start to take back some of the excessive controls that have been imposed by the Brussels dictators. It is arguable that any British political party can win the next election on the promise to address the restrictive practices imposed by the continental dictators, and demand a complete accounting of the money poured into this organisation.

Chapter Twenty Two
An Astro Analysis of The Death of Princess Diana.
Was this an accident, or was the Princess assassinated?

The world gasped when it was announced that Princess Diana had been killed in a car crash. Then reports came in thick and fast regarding her last moments, so that millions of people all over the world read every detail that was published in the press and on TV. We were informed that her driver was over the limit with alcohol, and that he also had a large percentage of carbon monoxide in his blood. The car was travelling at a great speed, and he lost control in the tunnel, which caused the crash.

Was this fact or fiction?

A white vehicle was seen inside the tunnel at the time of the crash but was never traced until years later. Before a statement could be obtained, the owner was found dead in his burnt-out car, and we were told that he had committed suicide.

How convenient?

The evidence given by the first person to arrive at the crash scene was totally suppressed by the French authorities. Why cover up important evidence?

The Princess was still alive when the ambulance arrived, then they drove very slowly passing two hospitals before arriving at their official destination. The distance to the nearest hospital should have been covered in less than ten minutes, yet it took over one hour to arrive at their official destination where the Princess subsequently died.

Who authorised the delay?

The tunnel where the accident occurred was examined by the French police, the car was removed, and the roadway was cleaned very early that same morning. Then the tunnel was re-opened, so any further possible forensic evidence was deliberately destroyed.

Who deliberately set out to destroy any possible evidence that could have been ascertained by a forensic analysis of the vehicle and the road conditions?

The Princess's body was embalmed before an autopsy was carried out even though this practice was forbidden in French law.
Who authorised this event and why? If this was a genuine accident, why have all the fine details been suppressed? Was it an accident or was the Princess assassinated? If so, why?

Firstly, it had been reported that the Princess wrote a letter, well before she died, saying that she felt her life was in danger, and that a car accident would be the most likely method. Probably she had some inside information about a previous arranged accident organized by the British Establishment.

Secondly, she travelled the world on behalf of numerous charities, behaving in a manner that was unacceptable to the British Royal Family, and the British Establishment. After her divorce from Prince Charles, she became far more popular than any other member of the Royal family, who appeared to be very aloof, so she would have made many enemies within the palace.

She undoubtedly upset the British Establishment, but that alone could not be the real reason for her demise. As Sherlock Holmes said in Conan Doyle's novels: Eliminate the impossible, and what is left, however improbable, must be the truth. Looked at from another angle, Princess Diana was psychologically an innocent, disturbed person, and she would have no idea of how the establishment really perceived her activities especially her romantic attachments.

If, for instance, she was involved with a person of a totally different religion, and if they produced a child, what would happen if the British Royal Family were assassinated en mass so that the conventional future heirs to the throne were eliminated?

Would it be possible for her child to ascend to the throne, and usurp the validity of the Church of England?
I am certain that the inner circle of power in Britain would never let that happen, and would eliminate any chance of such a revolution before it got under way. So if an accident was arranged, France would be the obvious choice because the judicial system stems from the time of Napoleon, and is vastly different to Britain. If the event had happened in

the British Isles, a team of top detectives would have descended on the location where the accident occurred, immediately sealing it off, and would subject every inch of space to a detailed examination, even if it took weeks and caused great disruption. Also, the vehicle would have been minutely examined, a public enquiry would have been announced, and the true facts very quickly ascertained.

However, it has taken years and much pressure by the media, for the French authorities to release even the smallest details of their investigations. The French were obviously in league with the British Establishment in an attempt to consign the true facts to the files of the official secrets act.
Why? Why? Why? What exactly do they want to keep secret from the Press and Public? Was it after all an accident, or was the vehicle tampered with?

Could the driver have been breathing in carbon monoxide from a small pipe attached to the exhaust, which could have been channelled into the car close to his face, so that the majority of the exhaust fumes found their way into his blood stream, and not into the other occupants of the car? Was a test done on the other victims to ascertain whether this was fact or fiction? Perhaps the car had been serviced only a very short time before the accident? Was there any investigation to find out whether that particular vehicle had been used by anyone else prior to the night in question?

Another interesting point is that an observer standing above the tunnel, heard what was described as an implosion, not an explosion, followed by an engine revving full blast, then a bang as the car hit a concrete post.

A Strange Experience

Let me tell you a very strange story that happened to me thirty years ago. I lived on a private estate where the gates are closed at the end of my avenue, so I had to enter the estate and turn along a narrow avenue road, usually parking almost right up against the locked gates. As I turned into the avenue, with the gates about two hundred yards away, I took my foot off the accelerator, and as I did so, the car shot away as though I had thrust my foot right down to the floor, yet I was not touching the accelerator pedal. For a couple of seconds I could not believe what was happening because the car was furiously accelerating towards the gates at an ever-increasing speed. I slammed in the clutch and braked furiously disconnecting the engine, which was by now going at about seven thousand revs per minute and still increasing. I switched off the ignition and managed to stop the car about two inches from the gates. If this type of accident could happen to me, which may have been fatal if I had not acted like lightning, could a similar event have occurred to the Princess's vehicle?

My car was not an automatic, so the technicalities between a gearbox with a standard clutch, and an automatic gearbox would probably be rather different. Not being an engineer, I would have no knowledge of whether the same fault could occur in an automatic gearbox. Could a small explosive device have been fitted to the Princess's car to interfere with the accelerator, which could have caused the initial implosion, then the noise of a high revving engine, followed by the sound of the actual crash? If I had not experienced a similar set of circumstances in my own vehicle, I would never have believed it was mechanically possible for such an event to happen.

Also why was the crashed vehicle spirited away and sealed off in a container without a complete examination by the Mercedes technicians? And if there was an examination of the wreck, why was it kept secret for so long?

All these questions need to be answered before a true verdict can be announced. Seventy percent of the British population believe it was not an accident, so if the cover-up is hidden away permanently in the files of the official secrets act we will never know the real answers to all my questions.

France must have the most questionable judicial system in Europe because important investigations regarding government officials are always heard in camera, and never released to the press and public. This system lends itself to absolute corruption, so what better place to hide the true facts of any so-called accident? No matter how much the establishment attempts to delay or bury the forensic evidence, the truth will eventually emerge! This is the law of cause and effect in operation, so the truth will come out in the end.

From an astrological point of view, the Princess's birth chart may throw some light on the subject. She was born on July 1st 1961 at 19.45 hrs Sandringham, England.

Sun   9 degrees 40 minutes in Cancer
Moon   25 degrees 2 minutes in Aquarius
Mercury   3 degrees 11 minutes in Cancer
Venus   24 degrees 24 minutes in Taurus   Retro
Mars   1 degree 39 minutes in Virgo
Jupiter   5 degrees 5 minutes in Aquarius   Retro
Saturn   27 degrees 48 minutes in Capricorn   Retro
Uranus   23 degrees 20 minutes in Leo
Neptune   8 degrees 38 minutes in Scorpio   Retro
Pluto   6 degrees 2 minutes in Virgo

North node of Moon 29 degrees 42 minutes Leo
South node of Moon 29 degrees 42 minutes Aquarius

Part of fortune 3 degree 47 minutes in Leo
Ascendant   18 degrees 25 minutes in Sagittarius
Midheaven   23 degrees 3 minutes in Libra

Planet Elements. Fire……….. 1
                  Earth……… 4
                  Air………… 2
                  Water………..3

Designation……..Cardinal……..3
              Fixed………...5
              Mutable……...2

On examining the Princess's dangerous planetary configurations at birth, the main characteristic is the T square of her Moon in Aquarius in her second house of finance, conjunct the south node of the Moon, which is where energy dissipates. The Moon in a woman's chart has particular influence on her emotional nature and health. Also, Uranus from Leo in her eighth house is in opposition, promoting sudden explosive unexpected events. This opposition is fuelled by an adverse aspect from Venus in Taurus, in her fifth house, ruling romance and love affairs; three areas all linking up with an adverse T square in fixed signs, which means that she was very determined to follow her own star at all costs. This aspect created a vast emotional turmoil right throughout her life, so once she made up her mind regarding any form of romance, she was immovable, regardless of any consequences. Then Mars ruling violence and accidents was conjunct Pluto the planet of death in Virgo operating from her eighth house of death, so at some time in life she could experience a sudden violent accident, which could be fatal.

Jupiter in Aquarius in her second house was adverse to Neptune in Scorpio in her tenth house, ruling her career within the Royal Family. So problems arose within the Royal Circle which were kept under wraps for many years.

Her best aspect was a Sun-Mercury conjunction in Cancer, in her seventh house of partnerships and marriage, in good aspect to her Pluto-Mars conjunction in Virgo, in her eighth house, and both were in good aspect to Neptune in Scorpio in her tenth house of career. This aspect means that she would eventually marry a famous person of note.

Saturn, the Planet of Fate

Saturn the great planet of fate was in Capricorn, in her first house, sending an excellent aspect to her natal Venus, ruler of Libra, but was adverse to her Libra-ruled Midheaven. These aspects influenced her work and career, so that her kind loving personality and artistic instincts were ground down with Royal Protocol, which she found stifling. Mars and Pluto conjunct in Mercury's sign of Virgo, ruling transport and communications, means that at sometime in her life, she could be involved in accidents while travelling.

Sagittarius, her ascendant or rising sign is ruled by Jupiter, so we have a very outgoing personality underneath the shy exterior that was often displayed in her early years. This area was in good aspect to her Moon-Uranus opposition, and could have helped to keep her alive if the accident had occurred in any other country except France. What we need now is to examine the Princess's progressed chart to find out whether any of these natal aspects were triggered or any adverse aspects occurred within the progressed chart.

Progressed Aspects

The major progressed aspects are that Uranus had moved two degrees and formed an exact opposition to her natal Moon, and a square aspect to her natal Venus, which together is a recipe for disaster promoting a sudden violent shock.

Then progressed Mercury was operating from 5 degrees and 50 minutes of Leo, in opposition to her natal Jupiter. The sixth degree of Leo is notorious for promoting blindness, not just eyesight, but also a general refusal to see what is in front of your nose. Mercury ruling transport and communications was operating from her eighth house of death; so an accident of some kind was on the cards. Her progressed Moon at 24 degrees 47 minutes was operating from her seventh house of partnerships, throwing a very good aspect to her natal Moon and progressed Uranus, which could have given her a greater chance for survival, if she had been transferred to the nearest hospital. Venus by progression was locked on to her natal Mercury at 3 degrees Cancer, so once again she received a very beneficial aspect, which could have been responsible for extending her life if she had received immediate treatment. Mars by progression was in Virgo, sending a great aspect to her natal Venus in Taurus; so once again we have a great protective aspect. Then to cap it all she had a couple of great aspects within her progressed chart, which was a 120-degree trine aspect from her progressed Mars to a conjunction of progressed Saturn and her progressed ascendant.

Now we come to the transiting planets on the day of her death

The transiting Sun and Mercury were conjunct in Virgo, joined to her progressed Pluto, planet of death, but in brilliant aspect to her natal Sun-Mercury conjunction and her natal Neptune. These aspects alone say that it was touch and go regarding her condition after the accident, and that perhaps she could have been saved in any other country where she would have been transported to hospital much faster. Mars was joined to her natal Neptune in Scorpio by two degrees in her tenth house, indicating a combination of illusion and violence. Mars rules violence and Neptune rules the world of drugs and illusions.

This is possibly the worst combination of aspects. Also Neptune at 27 degrees Capricorn was conjunct her natal Saturn, suggesting long-term planning could have been connected to this accident. With Uranus conjunct her natal Jupiter, in opposition to her progressed Mercury, and Pluto adverse to her natal Mars, her chances of living beyond this date were very slim.

Now we come to the final analysis of whether her death was an accident or was she assassinated? If it was a planned assassination, there is no better place to set it in motion because, the judicial system in France is so antiquated, where evidence is heard in camera, and has no place in a modern democratic society.

Evidence in France can legally be suppressed to suit the ruling government of the day.

There is only one conclusion, as Sherlock Holmes would say. If you eliminate the impossible, then whatever is left, no matter how improbable must be the answer. So if it was just a terrible accident, why has there been such a cover up of the vital evidence, and why has it taken so long for a public enquiry? This means that the British establishment wanted to hide this matter in the files of the official secrets act, hoping that the press and public will eventually accept their official verdict of accidental death.

All the evidence points to a well-planned assassination, otherwise the British establishment would have demanded and received a complete and open assessment of the facts which remain still hidden in 2006. If the establishment still covers up the evidence and consigns the details to the Official Secrets Act, this alone will be sufficient evidence for many people to prove that she was assassinated.

Chapter Twenty Three
"Tumo"
The ancient Tibetan art of internal body heat transference

The ancient Tibetan art of Tumo was originally designed by lamas, enabling them to keep warm in sub-zero conditions at high altitude. The Grand Master, and greatest exponent, was called Milerepo who it was said could dry forty blankets in one night. A soaking wet blanket was draped around his body, and by a great effort of mental concentration he could increase his body heat to such proportions that within a short space of time the blanket was dry.

Fact or fiction?

About twenty-five years ago I joined a martial arts group that originated in Tibet and practised a form of internal body heat transference. Unfortunately, this particular teaching only concentrated on the solar plexus which triggered the fire-ruled chakra without stabilising the lower water and earth ruled chakras. The effect of this practice was to throw many students off balance, mentally and emotionally. The system was later banned in Britain, and the Grand Master left for Indonesia, with the Customs and Excise, Inland Revenue, and the Police on his tail.

The Grand Master

The Grand Master developed an enormous following in Britain, and worked on the principle of grading people up to black belt in twelve months, then demanding that they set up their own teaching classes. The problem was that each instructor was responsible financially for setting up a class, and the profit was paid directly into the Grand Master's bank account without any remuneration for the instructors. We were also informed that we had to bring our classes to a central hall on a Saturday afternoon for extra training, which meant that the instructors and the students had to pay an extra fee to attend. Some students attended five classes per week, and some instructors ran the same number of classes without ever receiving a single penny for their effort and dedication. Once I realised the potential of this system, and started to become proficient myself, I fell foul of the hierarchy because I questioned the basic teaching principles. No one was taught that the basic principles were derived from the ancient Tibetan system of Tumo, so both instructors and students were left in the dark. As I was aware of the seven chakras, and had previously studied their purpose, I found myself teaching some of the principle instructors basic breathing techniques, to open up all seven chakras in the correct order, and then close them down at the end of a session. Since the dissolution of the organisation, I have developed and practised this ancient art of Tumo alone, so that my hands and feet never become cold, even in the severest weather.

The Breathing Exercises

By a series of exercises and breathing techniques combined, practised every day, and spread over a period of twelve months to two years, a student can become extremely proficient. The advantages are far greater than just keeping warm because the transference of internal body heat increases a practitioner's healing power. You can also remove any physical blockages within your own body, healing yourself much quicker than usual, keeping arthritic and rheumatic conditions at bay, or even curing them. It also promotes and develops your intuitive and psychic faculties so that you will eventually see the electrical force field being projected from the fingertips of an adept practitioner. I often hear of organisations offering to bring you up to master status in record time, but this of course is a total illusion because after twenty-five years of study and practice I still consider myself a student. Perhaps after another twenty-five years, I may get my foot on the bottom rung of the ladder for eventually becoming a master in the art of Tumo.

Defence against a Physical and Psychic Attack

I have also found Tumo of great help in dealing with a physical and psychic attack because the power released within can be quite awesome. As well as keeping yourself warm and physically fit, it promotes great physical and mental strength so that in a defensive situation you can transfer the internal body heat to your fists and feet, enabling you to deliver a most ferocious blow to your attacker. It can also protect you from serious harm should you receive a severe body blow, even directly to the solar plexus. I have a few friends who do not believe that I can take the most severe punches directly on my solar plexus without knocking me unconscious. However, grading for even the lower belts occurred only when a student could resist a brick being smashed into the solar plexus without injury, and at the higher levels, an Iron bar was used to strike the abdomen and back, in order to test the internal body heat protective envelope.

Evidence of Tumo in Operation

On one occasion I was in attendance at a grading as the official photographer, and there were around two hundred students in the hall seated cross-legged around the walls. One student was called into the centre where an instructor prepared to test him for his green belt. He was stripped to the waist, and stood with his legs well apart in order to obtain a good balance. The instructor felt his solar plexus to make sure that he was ready to take the brick. All seemed well, so the instructor placed the brick on his stomach then slowly swung it back and forth, while asking the student to concentrate then he swung the brick very hard and smashed it into the student's solar plexus. Having gone through this procedure myself, I had no problems when a brick was smashed into my abdomen but, unfortunately the student must have lost concentration at the last moment because he gasped for breath, his face turned a greyish green and he staggered back with a great bloody mark right across his abdomen. The instructor immediately called for the Vice Grand Master, who immediately placed one hand on the boy's back, and the other on his stomach covering the vivid red mark. I was about three feet away, and after only about two or three minutes I watched the red blotch slowly disappearing, until all that was left was a very slight red mark. No one else in the hall saw that instant healing at such close quarters. I knew then that internal body heat transference was much more than just keeping warm in cold conditions. Obviously you can never become an adept by reading an article or book but I can explain the basic principles, which will enable you to start the ball rolling.

The First Lesson

The first lesson is to light a candle then sit on the floor with your legs crossed Yoga style, or sit on a comfortable chair with your back upright, your feet touching, and your hands on your knees or clasped between your legs in order to close your circuit, so you do not lose energy. Concentrate on the tip of the candle flame. Breathe in slowly for about eight seconds, pushing your stomach out as far as it will go, hold your breath for eight seconds, then breath out just as slowly, only this time pull your stomach right in so you exhale the last drop of air from your lungs. Repeat this exercise for about five minutes while keeping your body as relaxed as possible. Check your neck and face muscles for tension, and continue deep breathing slowly in and out.

Concentration on the Root Chakra

Imagine a great golden energy directly from the Sun, glowing and pulsating, then entering your body through your nostrils with every breath. As you take in air visualise the energy travelling down your spine, right to the base. Here resides the Root Chakra ruled by the earth element. Hold your breath for eight seconds while concentrating on this lower area, and at the same time, visualise a giant oak tree with its roots going down your legs, anchoring you to the earth itself, then breathe out slowly, pushing out all your frustrations and negative energy.

The Sacral Chakra

Repeat this exercise seven times then on the next breath visualise the energy following the same path, but instead of remaining at the Root Chakra, click it up one notch to the Sacral Chakra, ruled by the water element which lies on your spine opposite your navel. Hold your breath and visualise energy activating this area before breathing out. Use any symbol you like such as a waterfall, river, the ocean or a still calm lake.

The Solar Plexus Chakra

The next area is the Solar Plexus Chakra, ruled by the fire element. Visualise a fireball travelling around your body and warming up your hands and feet. Once this chakra is developed, you will never suffer from cold hands and feet again.

The Heart Chakra

Next is the Heart Chakra, which is ruled by the air element. Visualise a cool summer breeze blowing through your body. The process starts with the oak tree, a stream nearby, warm sunlight filtering through the leaves of the oak tree, then a warm summer breeze. Each element of Earth, Water, Fire, and Air need to be well balanced within your etheric and astral body so that your physical body can function properly. If your earth chakra is not working properly, your skeleton structure will not be stable, and you may lack calcium and break or damage many bones during your lifetime. Also many decisions regarding your personal and business life will be made without using much common sense which the earth element supplies. You can build nothing of a permanent nature without the solid foundation of a well-balanced root chakra. The sacral chakra controls the water element, so if it is thrown out of balance, your lymphatic system controlling body fluids become blocked. It also affects all the other systems regulating the flow of body fluids, and when it becomes unbalanced you may experience crystallisation in the joints, resulting in rheumatism and arthritis. The Solar plexus chakra ruled by fire has particular reference to the digestive system, so if you ever suffer from chronic indigestion, or your hands and feet become very cold and numb in winter then this chakra is not balanced. Before any person ever feels the symptoms of a heart attack, the heart chakra closes down well in advance and is out of balance with the other chakras. This is then transferred from the astral to the physical, resulting in an arterial blockage. Above the lower chakras are the three higher elements starting with the throat chakra at the top of the spine, ruled by ether, which is the space that the lower four elements manifest through. There is particular reference here to the fixed sign of Taurus, which rules the throat area. You can always tell whether a throat chakra is well developed by the tone of voice because it is sound that rules here, so this is why a spoken mantra can help to balance the lower elements. In the beginning was the word, which is sound vibration. If the voice is articulate and balanced, the chakras are more likely to be vibrating in unison. If a person screeches or is inarticulate, the chakras will be unbalanced. Once you have balanced the four lower chakras, visualise energy entering through the nostrils, pausing for a moment at the root chakra, then clicking upwards, straight through the lower chakras before stopping at the throat chakra for eight seconds, before breathing out. The next area of concentration is your brow chakra, within your forehead, directly between the eyes. This is your third eye, so concentration here will develop your intuitive and psychic faculties enabling you to see and feel the internal body heat at work. One test of competence is practised with a partner standing back to back at a distance of six feet. One person directs the internal body heat to either the left, or right hand, the other partner tries to feel which hand is receiving the energy. The brow chakra is also the seat of power because whatever you visualise, and offer up to the light by repeated concentration, you can materialise. *As you think so you will become.* The seventh and final area is called the crown chakra, right at the top of your head, and when all the seven chakras are balanced and working like a well-oiled engine you will find it a steady source of strength and inner guidance.

The Secret of Perfect Health

The secret of perfect health in the physical world, and an understanding of the other dimensions, only arrive when you become emotionally and spiritually balanced. After opening up all seven psychic centres, your next step is to concentrate entirely on your solar plexus chakra and visualise a fireball travelling from your solar plexus, crossing up and over each shoulder simultaneously, and then rolling down your arms to your hands. Breathe in as before, then as you breathe half out, lock your solar plexus muscles, pushing across and down, then lock the muscles of your shoulders, upper and lower arms and finally clench your fists. Visualise the fireball travelling along the area of concentration, hold the tension for eight seconds, then relax all your muscles as you breathe out fully, and then start the process all over again. Having spent many years practising the transference of internal body heat, I now find that I can instantly project the energy to hands and feet, without going through the process of prolonged breathing. Now one of the most important and vital actions is to close down your chakras, all the way from the crown to the lower root chakra, before ending the session. Visualise wrapping each chakra up in a square of silk, from the crown right down to the root chakra so they are never left open after you have finished your meditation. Start following my instructions at the time of a New Moon, and if you practice for half-an-hour every day, you should start to feel results within three months or less, depending on your dedication, determination and concentration. To become really proficient, you will need at least two years' constant practice, and then you may never suffer from arthritis or need to wear gloves even in the coldest weather. This is the system that I use to obtain my greatest relaxation because when the exercises are completed, a state of utter relaxation occurs enabling me to slip out of the body more easily and start astral travelling. I will be following up this chapter with a complete book of instructions, showing you how to use the principles of Tumo in far greater detail, not only enabling you to keep warm in cold conditions, remove blockages in your physical body and promoting mental and physical health, but also to develop your skill as a healer, and enable you to defend yourself against sudden physical assault, and fight of a psychic attack. The title of my next book will be "Psychic and Physical Self Defence," and will be available in 2007. If you are interested, contact Trafford Publishing in advance of publication.

Chapter Twenty Four
A Modern Day Witch-Hunt

Most of us are aware of Arthur Miller's play "The Crucible" based on a true story of persecution in 1692 at Salem Massachusetts USA, where neighbours accused each other of witchcraft, and twenty men and women were executed because of jealousy and ignorance. Hysteria gripped the community so that if any neighbour had a dispute, they were accused of witchcraft. In those days people were tortured, hanged or burnt at the stake simply because they had a different perspective of the truth. How much have we progressed spiritually in over three hundred years? Judging by the national press when Glen Hoddle the England football coach was sacked amid a barrage of hate and prejudice for speaking his mind, and openly pronouncing his religious faith, we are undoubtedly still living in the dark ages!

Another Witch-Hunt in the USA

On February 22nd 1950, in Washington DC, Senator Joseph McCarthy announced that he had a list of two hundred-and-five names that were known to the Secretary of State as being members of the Communist party. So began a vast modern day witch-hunt, where many innocent people were ostracised and jailed. Ruthless people wishing to remove the opposition in government or work simply pointed a finger and growled 'Communist'. Such was the hysteria that people were continually in fear of losing their jobs or worse. It took until December 2nd 1954 before the Senate voted 67 to 22 to condemn Senator McCarthy for abusing his colleagues, and so ended that particular witch-hunt. In both cases, those in power removed freedom of speech, and severe punishment was dished out to individuals who had the courage to speak up for their beliefs.

Two thousand years ago the authorities of the day crucified a man called Jesus because he claimed he was the Son of God. "I and the Father are one and the same," he said, which was one of the excuses they needed under the guise of blasphemy, to do the dark deed. It seems that we haven't learnt much from his sacrifice or his great teachings. "In my Father's House there are many Mansions," he said. Substitute "Universe" for "my Father's House", and "dimensions" for "mansions" and you have a modern-day interpretation of what Jesus could have meant. So how come we are still so ignorant regarding the world of spirit, and conduct modern-day witch-hunts? On Lamas day the 2nd February 1999, the headlines in the Daily Express were "Game's Up For Hoddle." Eight out of ten readers say: "England's manager must go". Ian Gallagher wrote "Glen Hoddle defied public opinion yesterday by refusing to quit over his 'offensive' comments about disabled people." Even Tony Blair stated that Hoddle's remarks were very offensive, and it would be difficult for him to stay. Margaret Hodge, Minister for the Disabled, called for him to go, and when interviewed on TV she stated that Hoddle's remarks helped to focus media attention on the disabled, which was what she had been attempting to do as the Minister for the disabled; so she was delighted to climb on board the band wagon, condemning the England coach. James Stracken, chief executive for the Royal National Institute for the Deaf said: "Hoddle's remarks were ridiculous, and belonged to the dark ages."

It was not Hoddle's remarks that belonged to the dark ages but it was the ignorance of the critics. Neil Betteridge of Radar, the Royal Association for Disability and Rehabilitation said: "Hoddle's remarks were grossly offensive to disabled people, and that they should have the same rights as everyone else." What on earth has a person's rights got to do with whether or not they are disabled? Mencap were also just as totally prejudiced. Psychologist Dr. George Sik was reported to have said, "Hoddle's beliefs did not correspond to any accepted doctrine." What he meant was that Glen Hoddle's remarks did not coincide with his personal philosophy. Did the so-called enlightened newspapers reporting offensive comments about Glen Hoddle realise that by their rude comments they were offending half the world's population, by their ignorance of reincarnation, and the law of Karma?

Both the Hindu and Buddhist religions are based on reincarnation, and have absolute faith in the words "As we sow, we will reap," which is also a Christian concept taught by Jesus. The truth is that possibly ninety percent of the world's people are disabled, not physically or mentally, but spiritually. Look around this planet and witness the violence and bloodshed going on every day. There are wars everywhere, with torture, murder and people starving whilst the fat cats get richer every day. The Gulf war started because they could not let Saddam Hussein control the oil revenue, so the west intervened. When the Chinese invaded Tibet, the western politicians turned their backs because there was no oil in Tibet, and China was a great source of revenue for western goods and armaments. House repossessions and business bankruptcies during the last fifteen years is offensive and immoral. Just because of a job loss, or a miscalculation of finances, the banks and building societies carry out another kind of witch-hunt, by throwing people out of their homes, and closing down small businesses when they really needed money to keep going. It would be very simple to allow a family in financial trouble to either keep their houses and pay off the mortgage over a longer period, or allow them to retain possession, and pay a rental that they can afford, until the mortgage has been paid. One friend lived in a London flat for thirty years with her mother and daughter, and when the mother died, because the tenancy was in the mother's name, the Landlord sent a letter doubling the rent before the body had left the house. Without a belief in reincarnation, the behaviour of the human race makes no sense. When I was young, I realised that Shakespeare knew a thing or two about the other dimensions, with the quote from Hamlet to Horatio, on the battlement of the castle. *"There are more things in heaven and earth Horatio than are dreamt of in your philosophy."*

Have the people condemning Hoddle never heard those famous lines and thought about their inner meaning? Why should the majority of people totally misunderstand the message that Hoddle was trying to put over? He was not in any way denigrating the disabled, he was trying to offer them comfort by way of an explanation for their physical and mental problems.

This is a classic example of modern day witch-hunting, where the ignorant in their so-called wisdom are prepared to castigate an innocent person because they have a different belief. This is where the term "Political Correctness" is used to destroy a person's reputation because he does not fit in to the accepted mould. This abominable description can be summed up very neatly when recently I heard a very well known personality talking about the black and white minstrels who blacked up their faces for stage and TV performances. He then mentioned that Al Jolson, who also blacked up his face when performing, was politically incorrect and racist. When Al Jolson died, tens of thousands of black actors, singers, dancers, musicians and ordinary people lined the route taken by his coffin, to pay their respects to their hero, who had blacked up his white face to sing his immortal melodies. If it is racism for Al Jolson to black up his face, what do the woolly-minded do-gooders make of Michael Jackson, permanently whitening his face, or Lenny Henry appearing in a film with his face whitened? What sort of mind says it is fine for a black man to whiten his face, but it is racism if a white man blacks his face when appearing on stage? Also, what about all the performers and presenters on TV that use brown make-up, to make themselves look more presentable in front of the cameras? Is every person on TV a racist because they change the colour of their skin by using make-up? Is Boy George a racist, just because he wears powerful make-up and outrageous costumes when performing on stage or on TV?

"Those whom the Gods destroy, they first make mad," has never been a more apt description of the present-day human race.
Dictatorial people only use the words "Politically Correct" in order to influence others to follow their specific pathway with the object of domination, which really means that your personal freedom of speech is being eroded at every opportunity by these bullying tactics. Next time you hear those words, ask the perpetrator to explain, and you will find that they have no real answer. They just repeat the words like a parrot without ever thinking of the true meaning. "Political Correctness and Racism" go hand in hand. Now the bigots are about to stop people smoking in public places, in the belief that it is a health hazard. Yet they allow vast pollution from diesel and petrol engines to pollute the atmosphere in far greater quantities than a million smokers can produce. The bigots breathe in these toxic fumes, and ignore the less dangerous tobacco smoke. They constantly tell us that different types of food are dangerous but never tell the public that many of the drugs prescribed by doctors and hospitals create various after effects, which could in the long run be more dangerous than the illness that they are supposed to prevent. Why should any government interfere with what we eat? Who has the right to tell me what I should eat, or whether I should or should not smoke tobacco. Yet governments do nothing about the really dangerous drug culture, letting pushers infect school children with numerous hard drugs from a very early age. Now they are conducting a campaign about drinking too much alcohol. Obviously, if you drink too much booze you could end up like George Best with a liver implant. As an exercise, examine the behaviour

pattern of your friends and relatives, and after observation and analysis of what they say and do, have a go at predicting the outcome of their health pattern by applying the Law of Karma, and see what you find. It is so easy to pinpoint people, who are going to be in trouble in the future, and by the future I do not mean next month or year because it sometimes takes years for the great law of cause and effect to operate, but it never fails. This is what Glen Hoddle was trying to say to the public in order to help comfort those who were physically and mentally afflicted, giving them reason and hope for the future, but the un-evolved bigots who jumped to a personal conclusion will eventually pay the price for their abysmal ignorance of the laws of God.

What governments forget is that they can fool the people most of the time, but they can never fool all the public all of the time. Eventually out of one of the great universities will emerge a new breed of politician who will set up a completely new party by offering the public a manifesto based on reducing taxes, and making all government departments account for every penny they spend. They will hand back to the people of Britain the right to govern themselves, by eliminating all the control lines imposed by the EEC, and the New Fascist Labour Government.

Instead of pumping more money into the health service, why not reduce the massive number of top-heavy administrators, and increase the medical staff then bring in more modern equipment? Why not cut back on the vast amount of unnecessary drugs, and integrate natural complementary medicine? This would save billions, but the drug companies and the people with a vested interest will resist this suggestion with all their might. Why not also hold back the billions of pounds that the EEC dictators pump into the pockets of French landowners under the guise of the Common Agricultural Policy? The black hole of the EEC's finances will eventually have to be brought out in to the open. Then the excessive money that we give to the Brussels Commissars could be used to finance British roads, railways, the National Health Service, and reduce taxes all round. Kill the ridiculous controls that Brussels apply and reverse all their attempts to control the British population. We should stay in Europe as a completely independent nation, trading together without restrictions and eliminate the vast overspending, and taking back our billions of pounds that they waste every year. We could spend that money on the British economy, rather than allow un-elected bigots to dictate how we spend our money. Unless great changes occur in the EEC, especially within the "Common Agricultural Policy," it will all end in tears because, the law of Karma never fails, and even though it may take many years before the true financial facts are uncovered. The rules, controls, and regulations pumped out by the politicians are simply a modern day witch-hunt, designed to increase their control of the population. In Britain, we let criminals out of prison to commit further atrocities because the woolly-minded liberals are more concerned with the human rights of the criminals than the law abiding citizens. Now the New Fascist Labour Government is planning to use satellite navigation to keep track of motorists. Where will it all end? What will be the future of the Human Race? Will we become redundant on planet Earth like the Dinosaurs? Or will we develop spiritually and colonise the outer planets, or even the distant stars? It all depends on how balanced we become during the next few hundred years.

The Scales of Justice

Just imagine a giant set of scales. One side is occupied by the violent, ruthless, egotistical, controlling section of humanity. On the other side are people who follow the path of love, light and compassion regardless of their own personal religion. The volume of thought formed from both sides will create the final judgement. If the majority of people follow the Cathar Prophesy, written in the first chapter of this book, the Human Race will survive. But if the controlling, ruthless and violent ones dominate then Mother Earth will eventually spit out fire and brimstone, wiping us all off the face of the planet. Then life will start from scratch all over again, just like it did sixty-five million years ago, with possibly another species rising from the ashes. I hope that this book will make you think more deeply about the possibility that a "Multi Dimensional Universe" really exists, not just in my imagination because each and every one of us has at some time experienced close contact with another dimension. Fear and prejudice often prevents most people from analysing psychic events in a scientific manner. Open your mind to the reality of life, and go forward into the light. "Blessed Be."

Sources of Reference

The A to Z Horoscope Maker and Delineator by Llewellyn George is an American textbook published by Llewellyn Publications. This is probably the finest source of reference available today, even though it was first published in 1910.
Aleister Crowley. The Complete Astrological Writings. Published by Tandem Books. A great source of reference.
The Tarot by Alfred Douglas. Published by Penguin books. This has been a great source of information, and is a must for any student of the Tarot.
The Book of World Horoscopes by Nicholas Campion. Published by the Aquarian Press. An excellent reference book covering horoscopes of countries and political parties.
Heart Ailments Produced by The Science of Life Books, Australia. Details out the true value of Vitamin E for heart conditions.
Fate Magazine Now ceased publication, but I have probably 240 volumes, printed over twenty years, covering almost every subject within the paranormal.
Prediction Magazine. I have a similar number of volumes from this monthly publication during the time that Madeline Montalban, Alfred Douglas and Jo Sheridan wrote most of the articles. I have also written a number of articles for this magazine.
The Occult by Colin Wilson. Published by Hodder and Stoughton.
Any book by Colin Wilson is worth reading
The Hand and the Horoscope by Fred Gettings Published by Hamlyn
The author combines astrology and palmistry
TV programmes, national newspapers and the web are a great source of information for any writer. I always make notes from any programme that is broadcast, and cut out information from newspapers for future reference.
The World Greatest UFO Mysteries. by Nigel Blundell and Roger Boar. Published by Octopus Books. One of the best UFO books available.
The Higher Power You Can Use. by Macdonald-Bayne.
Published by L.N. Fowler & Co Ltd.
The Chakras by Peter Rendel. Published by The Aquarian Press.
Raphael's Astronomical Ephemeris
Published by W. Foulsham & Co Ltd

Astrological information can be obtained from the web site www.stella-vision.co.uk covering business astrology with dates of possible stock market crashes in 2007. Also a basic Jupiter chart showing the actual dates that the great planet of luck and abundance makes a direct aspect to any birthday during the autumn of 2006 and right through 2007.

ISBN 1412099940-4